d in Nashville, Tennessee, by Thomas Nelson. Thomas Nelson is a registered trademark of Nelson, Inc.

nanagement by KLO Publishing Service.

Nelson, Inc., titles may be purchased in bulk for educational, business, fund-raising, or sales onal use. For information, please e-mail SpecialMarkets@ThomasNelson.com.

of Congress Control Number: 2009938235

78-0-7852-2157-9

Printed in the United States of America
10 11 12 13 14 RRD 6 5 4 3 2

BUSINESS WITH SOUL

BUSINES[S] WITH SOU[L]

CREATING A WORKPLACE RICH IN FAITH A[ND]

MICHAEL CARDON[E]

THOMAS NELSON
Since 1798

NASHVILLE DALLAS MEXICO CITY RIO D[E]

Publi
Thon

Proje

Thon
prom

Unles
1982

Scrip
1996

Scrip
Publi

Libra

ISBN

Contents

Acknowledgments vii
Tribute to My Family ix
Introduction: Creating a Business with Soul xi

1. At Our Core 1
2. A Triple Bottom Line 13
3. Give Your Business to God 21
4. The Ministry of Business 30
5. In Pursuit of Excellence 41
6. Creating a Business "Family" 50
7. Helping People Develop 62
8. Three Traits for the Job 73
9. The Search for Significance 83
10. Making Factory Space a Special Place 91
11. Urgency Plus Persistence 100
12. Establishing Two-Way Communication 106
13. A Factory with Chaplains 121
14. A Job Description Rooted in Caring 133
15. Crossroads: The Intersection of Faith and Work 142
16. Exceeding Customer Expectations 147
17. A Company That Gives 158
18. Cultivating Servant Leadership 166
19. The Seven Choices Servant Leaders Make 175
20. Recipients of a Legacy . . . and Passing It On 186
21. Define Yourself, Define Your Company 198
22. Two Key Leadership Issues 205
23. The Challenges Ahead 213

Notes 222

Acknowledgments

Many more people could and probably should be included in this book, because my personal success and our corporate growth are the result of the efforts of the many great people who have surrounded me and greatly impacted my life.

My wife, Jacquie, first and foremost, gets the most credit for her support and loving input into my life, along with our children, Michael III, Christin, and Ryan, who literally grew up with our business. I so appreciate and remember my mom and dad, who patiently raised and worked with me in founding CARDONE Industries.

Mark Spuler and his family have been alongside for all these years. Without Mark's efforts this book would not have been written.

Randy Elliott's encouragement, wisdom, and patient advice have kept this book alive.

Steve Rabey and Jan Dargatz were also of great assistance during this writing.

For all those who are a part of CARDONE Industries, past and present, there could be stories included of your great contributions to this ongoing saga. Whenever a group of us get around a table, new stories and old names always seem to emerge as we recount our amazing past, the sacrifices made, and the growth we continue to experience. Your great contributions are well remembered. Thanks to all of you.

To God be the glory, great things He has done!

TRIBUTE TO MY FAMILY

Throughout the book you will read about our Factory Family, the people who operate and lead our business. "Family" is a concept that comes from the Bible, where it says, God is our Father and Jesus is God the Son. I believe the term *Family* applies first and foremost to our personal families. I do not believe you can be a true servant leader if you don't make it your first priority to serve your own family. I have known well-intentioned and successful people in business and ministry who have put their careers and businesses ahead of their families, resulting in tragic relationships. I attribute our corporate success to a commitment I made to my personal family first. For me, success in business starts at home. Making time for sports, meal times, and together time is critical to family harmony. My commitment to my family was that if they ever thought my career or our business was taking priority before them, I would leave the business.

I give the credit for balancing family and business first to my wife, Jacquie. Her honest feedback and wisdom have kept me on track. Jacquie's role in the success of the business as cofounder started on day one, and continues to her role today as Mom, Mimi, and CARDONE Industries board member. Credit also goes to my children, Michael III and his wife, Alexandra; to Christin and her husband, Dan; and to Ryan and his wife, Christian, for their great support. They had the extra burden of being the *family* of the family business. It has been said that when you have a family business you have more than just a family.

INTRODUCTION

Creating a Business with Soul

While you may not have heard of CARDONE Industries, the company my father and mother, my wife, Jacquie, and I founded in 1970, there's a good chance you or someone you know has used one of our high-quality automotive products. More than two hundred million of our products have helped people keep their cars and trucks on the road.

In the pages that follow you will learn about our family-owned company, which employs more than five thousand people in the United States, Canada, Mexico, and Europe in the remanufacturing of automotive service parts for millions of vehicles around the world. More than that, I hope you will learn what it means to me to be a businessperson with an integrated faith in God as seen in my work, my strong motivation to succeed, and my commitment to helping people. In these pages you will see how my career is marked by a threefold passion for life, work, and faith. I hope what you read will inspire you to live a life of even greater significance, forging a career that is worthy of your time, energy, and passion. Just picking up this book to read says something about your interest as a leader in creating a business and living your life with a faith dimension.

If a person like me, who graduated fifty-ninth out of sixty

students in his high school class can start, grow, and lead a global company, you can too! Far more than a sense of accomplishment, however, I have found a deep sense of purpose and meaning for my life. I have far exceeded my expectations, and you can too.

Most of the people I know want to make a difference in the world. They want to find joy, meaning, fulfillment, and satisfaction in their work. What has made the difference for me is my desire to win by being the *best* at what I do. To me, winning in business means running a highly profitable business and growing it as large as it can grow. At the same time and without any compromise, I believe winning involves merging my faith in God with the work of my hands.

Deep within, I know I am a "businessman with a soul," and as a natural extension of myself, I want to create a "business with soul." This book tells you how my family and I set out to accomplish that goal personally and professionally.

The methods shared in these pages have worked for us. Today, we are the largest privately owned remanufacturer of auto parts in the world. We are at the cutting edge in a hypercompetitive global market. We have documentation for the ways in which we have improved the quality of life for our employees, customers, suppliers, and community. We give a healthy and consistent return on investment to our shareholders. We contribute generously to the economic and community life of Philadelphia, as well as the other communities in which our business operates. We have a thirty-nine-year "track record." Like our automotive parts, our biblically based principles and practices have been road-tested under intense competitive pressure and in challenging business environments. These principles and practices have demonstrated their practicality and resilience time and again. They have given us purpose and results and have been the catalyst for our growth from a mom-and-pop operation to a global enterprise.

And yet, we continue to wrestle with ways to improve our work and our business by drawing more deeply from the well of God's infinite wisdom. We look to Him as the greatest Source of creativity and innovation in our universe. We make no claim to having "arrived." We do make a claim to being highly focused and intentional about where we are going and how we pursue excellence in all things. We are driven to maintain a strong sense of purpose as our company continues to grow.

Although our purpose-driven methods are effective for us, we're the first to admit our way is not the only way to integrate faith and work. Consequently, I encourage you to experiment and explore ways you can integrate your faith and work. As you read this book, my hope is you will be stimulated to reevaluate the meaning of your life, the purpose of your work and career, the motives that drive you, the dynamic tension between right and wrong, competitiveness and compassion, profit and charity, good and evil, and a host of other "life" issues related to doing business and living well.

For years I searched for a management approach that would not only work for me personally, but could be adopted company-wide by every employee—for the benefit of every employee—regardless of his or her position. Through my friend Ken Blanchard, coauthor of *The One Minute Manager*, I encountered the "Servant Leadership" model, which is based on the life of Jesus Christ. I am convinced this is the most appropriate leadership model for CARDONE Industries. Through the years I have seen this leadership model not only take root and grow in our company, but also produce amazing results—financially and interpersonally.

Although the Bible doesn't say anything about brakes or wiper motors, it does tell us about Jesus and how His approach to leadership has impacted the world for more than two thousand years. The Bible and my relationship with Jesus give me purpose and meaning in both my business and personal life. The Servant Leadership of Jesus Christ has become the leadership model for me personally and for my business. I am convinced God has meaningful input for our lives and has a personal plan that can bring the fulfillment and purposeful direction we desire, whatever our work may be.

I

At Our Core

Identifying an Unshakable Center from Which Business and Life Decisions Can Flow

Every business or enterprise has a core of some type. It may be their core reason for being a business, making a core product, or addressing a core concern. The core of a business may be stated or unstated, but it exists nonetheless.

At CARDONE, we have another definition for the word *core*. First, *core* is the term we use in our remanufacturing industry for our basic raw material. The core is a used auto part we remanufacture in our plants. But our real core, the core of our business, is comprised of the well-defined values and objectives from which our decisions flow. We are intent upon creating a corporate culture, a core, based on values that give meaning to our work while driving and defining our business.

CREATING A VALUES-BASED CORPORATE CULTURE

Any person who has ever traveled, whether it's to the other side of a large city or around the world, has seen firsthand the diversity and power of culture. Culture is why people in the industrialized world wear clothes to work, instead of bearskins, fig leaves, or nothing at all! Culture is why business people shake hands in Philadelphia, bow to one another in Tokyo, and kiss each other on the cheek when meeting in Rome. Culture is why we get goose bumps when we hear the "Battle Hymn of the Republic" or take our children to a fireworks display on the Fourth of July.

Anthropologists define culture as the patterned ways human beings in different places organize both their personal lives and their societies. Anyone who ever ventured beyond the front door of his own home knows that culture varies widely from one place to another.

The same is true for companies. Each company has its own "corporate culture." There is a pattern to the way each company organizes, thinks, and operates. At the core of the business culture are the *values* that become the framework for the behaviors and actions of its people.

Some companies are up-front about their "corporate-culture values." For example, Google highly values employee creativity, and in turn, gives generous cash rewards for new ideas. Starbucks values small-scale enterprises, and in turn, buys coffee beans from small indigenous growers.

Other companies are less up-front about their corporate culture and values. But each company has values, stated or unstated, that influence the way it operates, impact the work environment, and affect the morale of its employees.

There are several questions about corporate cultures, which I find most interesting.

- Is the corporate culture intentional?

- Is it a by-product of planning and training, or does it evolve and develop by accident?
- Who creates the corporate culture?
- What principle or philosophy forms the foundation for the corporate culture?
- Who is responsible for perpetuating the corporate culture?

At CARDONE, we believe culture must be addressed directly and that the family members and leaders within the business have the primary responsibility for creating, modeling, and being the gatekeepers of our business culture. We are very intentional about defining our corporate values and we are equally intentional about making certain these values are cultivated at all levels of our organization. Our values are written and ranked in order and made widely known throughout our business. These values are taught to our new Factory Family Members. At every level, we remind ourselves of what we believe and what we are striving to do. We are determined that our values and corporate culture will drive our business, not the other way around.

> *"I believe wholeheartedly that when the right things are done for the right reasons, a company reaps incredible results."*
> —MICHAEL CARDONE JR.

Having devoted significant resources to articulating, training, and reinforcing our core values, we spend a great deal of energy finding new ways to express these values through our relationships with our customers, vendors, and the community at large. We do this because we know a distinctive, powerful corporate culture doesn't just happen. Leaders must be intentional about creating the culture their business reflects.

At CARDONE, we do not have a budget line item entitled "Corporate Values." Rather, our corporate values provide the framework for our every action, behavior, policy, and procedure.

VALUES ROOTED IN FAITH

We make no apology that the foundation of our corporate culture springs from our faith in God and the Servant Leadership model of Jesus as documented in the Bible. At the same time, it is our faith that leads us to apply our values in very practical ways to the benefit of all in our company, whether an employee shares our faith or not. There are two principles I believe are essential in this area.

First, model what you want to see in others. Creating a viable, distinctive, and powerful corporate culture based on faith and values requires far more than plaques on a wall or statements made in training programs and strategic plans. Creating corporate culture requires embodying key values in everything we do. I believe that a lack of top leadership support for corporate values is the number-one threat to undermining the corporate culture we have created. Therefore, I make it a personal priority to consistently model the attitudes and behaviors I want to see around me and I seek to hire and develop people who are willing to do the same.

We all know people who talk the talk but don't walk the walk. Those who say one thing and do another make it impossible to create a consistent corporate culture. Employees and customers know the difference between superficial platitudes and seriously embraced corporate values. We want to walk the talk. I want what

I do and what I believe to be congruent. Therefore, I try not to act in a way that is out of alignment with my values.

One of our team leaders came to our Director of Training to request Servant Leadership training for the people working under him. Our Director of Training reminded the team leader that Servant Leadership is not something people can learn in a classroom. Servant Leadership must be taught by example. Team members have to see you as a servant leader, who models what he is teaching.

Second, do what's right. Doing the right thing means acting in alignment with your core values. This isn't a luxury. It is a necessity. The culture we are creating and reinforcing requires it.

Perhaps the most difficult time to do the "right" thing in business is when doing the right thing seemingly costs more than not doing the right thing. In 1982, Johnson & Johnson found itself in the spotlight after seven people, who had taken Extra-Strength Tylenol capsules, died as a result of cyanide poisoning. The company initially recalled a few lots of Tylenol capsules. Then, at a cost of $31 million, it ordered a nationwide recall of all Tylenol bottles. In hindsight, the nationwide recall wasn't necessary, but Johnson & Johnson leaders knew it was the *right* thing to do in order to maintain the trust of its consumers and the physicians who recommend their products. When faced with this decision, the leadership at McNeil Pharmaceutical of Johnson & Johnson went back to the company's mission statement for the answer. Within the Johnson & Johnson credos you will find these statements:

> We believe our first responsibility is to the doctors, nurses and patients, to mothers and fathers and all others who use our products and services. In meeting their needs

> everything we do must be of high quality . . . We must provide competent management . . . and their actions must be just and ethical. We are responsible to the communities in which we live and work and to the world community as well.

Though the decision to recall Tylenol capsules was costly, Johnson & Johnson remained true to its values and further reinforced its corporate culture. The action taken by Johnson & Johnson was totally consistent with what the company claimed to be at its core.

At CARDONE we faced a similar challenge that put our values to a test. One of the nation's leading auto parts distributors came to us and asked us to produce an entire product line of low-cost auto parts that they wanted to carry in their three thousand–plus stores. The opportunity looked inviting and the potential sales they submitted to us were significant. One of our corporate objectives is "to grow profitably," so just as we do with all new opportunities, we began to analyze, discuss, and pray about this. We did our internal cost projections and shared our findings with the customer. We concluded we could not produce the products they wanted at their price without compromising our corporate objectives and values. So, we turned down their offer. Of course, we were disappointed to lose the business, but it was for the right reason. The customer was thoughtful enough to give us the news they were changing suppliers and going with our competitor for this product line at 30 percent lower prices than we had quoted.

After we received the news, we called our team together to let them know about our customer's decision to take their business elsewhere. Though it was a costly decision on our part, we had remained true to our core values.

Over the next two years, the wisdom of our prayerful and consistent decision was revealed. The competing company, which had agreed to produce the new product line, was unable to fulfill its contract in a timely and profitable manner. This competitor underestimated its costs and eventually went out of business. The customer returned to us and, once again, began buying large quantities of parts.

Tough decisions don't always produce immediate short-term profits, and not all decisions will turn around as this one did, but consistently basing actions on right values does pay off in the long term. I have no doubt about that.

Tests of your values and objectives *will* come. Look for them and recognize them as defining moments and as the "values" challenges they are. Your response will strengthen or weaken the foundation of your corporate culture and impact the core of your business.

FRAMING VALUES IN WORDS

For values to take root and grow, they must be communicated. This means they must be clearly stated.

CARDONE is based on its values. Our vision, mission, objectives, and values are not the exercise of a corporate retreat or mere credos. The values on the next page permeate our individual lives, characterize our leadership, and give meaning to all we do in business. Our goal in leadership is to influence and model these statements. If you want to know what is at the core of CARDONE, read the following statements and know that we not only take them seriously, but these statements reflect the very substance of our lives.

Our Mission
To be the best
remanufacturer
in the world

***Our Objectives**
To honor God in all we do
To help people develop
To pursue excellence
To grow profitably

Our Values
We value our people
We value our work
We value our witness
We value our word

Our Foundation
The Servant Leadership Model
"Whoever wants to be great among you
must be your servant."
- Jesus
Humility - Confidence - Resolve - Influence

Our leadership model is the Servant Leadership modeled by Jesus Christ.

We believe the greatest leader who ever lived is Jesus Christ. While this may seem like a religious statement, religion isn't why we look at Jesus as the model servant leader. We think of Jesus' leadership in this way:

- Jesus lived more than two thousand years ago.
- He modeled Servant Leadership by washing people's feet.

* Years ago I received verbal permission from C. William Pollard, Chairman of The ServiceMaster Company, to use his company's objectives as our own since they so well fit what I believed should be the objectives of Cardone Industries.

- He was a teacher, not a political leader.
- His public career was only three years.
- He trained and developed twelve successors.
- He is the only leader who died for His people instead of asking His people to die for him.
- He gave the world a powerful message of love and grace that effectively and positively changes lives.
- His influence continues to impact our world two thousand years later.

Look at any leadership book from among those on the bestseller lists and ask yourself: Will this leader be known two thousand years from now? The Servant Leadership modeled by Jesus is a model that teaches us how a person might effectively influence other people in a positive way. Every person in our company is challenged to serve others and to put others first. Every person in our company is challenged to live out our core values in ways that influence, support, and encourage others to be their best and to give their best by inspiring others to seek excellence in every area of life. Every person who aspires to lead is encouraged to study, grow, and develop in Servant Leadership.

OUR COMMITMENT TO RELIGIOUS FREEDOM
(How We Balance Faith-Based Values and Individual Free Will)

As a family-owned company, we embrace biblical values. We also celebrate the religious and cultural diversity of our thousands of employees. We believe in the inherent dignity, respect, and free will of all people, which was modeled by Jesus. We respect every person, regardless of his or her race, color, religion, or national origin. "Leading like Jesus" has nothing to do with religion; it has everything to do with how a person serves and works with others.

COMMUNICATING VALUES THROUGHOUT THE COMPANY

Corporate value statements lose their effectiveness if they do not permeate all levels of an organization and influence everything that is done. How can a company ensure that its values have a trickle-down effect that ultimately influences every person?

Before answering that question, there are a couple of things we must acknowledge. First, business leaders cannot dictate behavior. Although leaders can set the standards and model behavior, there is no way one can ensure all corporate objectives and values are impacting every person in the organization equally. Second, conveying values boils down to communication, communication, and communication.

There are a number of very practical ways by which we communicate our values at CARDONE:

Plaques on the Walls. In all of our meeting rooms, which we call "Decision Rooms," statements of our objectives and values are framed and placed in full view. These statements are regular reminders of what we want to achieve.

Banners and Posters Displayed in Every Plant. These serve as constant reminders of the things we consider to be of paramount importance.

E-mails to Our Key Leaders. Through e-mail we connect our Factory Family to the real-time issues and events impacting our business. These are short, pithy, single-topic messages related to business conditions and our culture. Through these e-mail messages we communicate our values and stimulate conversations around our values.

Voice Mails. Weekly, thematic voice mail messages are sent to our Factory Family Members. These messages are short, to the point, and reinforce our values.

W.O.W. Meetings. We have regular "Workers of Worth" (W.O.W.) meetings. In these large group gatherings we review business performance, recognize our employees, celebrate excellence, and communicate essentials relating to our industry and competition.

Newsletters. We publish monthly wellness newsletters, which highlight different health and general life topics.

Daily "Take 5" Meetings. We have daily small-group meetings throughout the factories and offices at the beginning of each workday. These meetings are called "Take 5." During this time, we convey practical information and include an inspirational message related to who we are as a business.

One-on-One Meetings. These meetings are a vital component of Servant Leadership, creating an environment where open communication can take place between leaders and employees. In these sessions, leaders provide coaching and support for our employees and seek to become aware of employee concerns. Goals and priorities are aligned and progress is monitored.

NO APOLOGY FOR VALUES

We make no apology for holding and upholding the values that we, as a family, have developed and lived out over the years at CARDONE. We hold fast to these values, because we know they work! They are the foundation stones on which we have built a successful and growing company. The values we espouse as leaders of this company are a seamless extension of who we are as individuals.

While we do not expect or require our customers and vendors to know and adopt our values, we constantly strive to communicate our values to them through our behavior, products, and service. We don't brandish our value statements in our advertising, product boxes, or business cards, but we do print our Mission Statement on our business cards: "To be the Best Remanufacturer in the World." We want others to know what they can expect from us and why they can expect it from us, even though they may not share our values. Whenever I am asked what makes CARDONE tick, my reply is, "our core values."

QUESTIONS ONLY YOU CAN ANSWER

1. What are the values on which your company or organization is founded?
2. What results are being produced from these values?
3. How are your company's values communicated?
4. How do your personal values relate to your company's values?
5. Can you cite a situation that tested and helped define your company's values? Your personal values?

2

A Triple Bottom Line

"Profitable" Can Mean More than "Making a Profit"

We are not unlike other businesses in our attention to "the bottom line." When Wall Street analyzes a business, they focus on the bottom line. Business leaders want to know how decisions will impact the bottom line.

If you type the phrase "bottom line" into a powerful Web site search engine, you will get more than fifty-five million Web site matches! When you consider the various definitions of "the bottom line," they go beyond business applications. People apply this powerful expression to everything from personal decision making to international foreign policy.

In common language, a company's financial bottom line sums up the activities and efforts of an organization over a period of time. The most simplified financial statement considers a company's net revenues minus expenses and taxes. Whatever is left over after expenses and taxes is considered the net income or the "bottom line."

At CARDONE, we view this financial definition as only one part of the bottom line. We see our business as having a greater purpose than just our financial bottom line. Just as any person is more than a financial entity, so is our business. In addition to the financial aspect, we regard our business as having spiritual and social elements. Our triple bottom line has financial, spiritual, and social dimensions, requiring us to evaluate every future decision and every process in light of the people associated with our company, including our employees, customers, vendors, and the communities impacted by our business. We have found balancing the financial, social, and spiritual elements, which comprise our overall bottom line, has a synergistic effect that positively impacts both today's results and the future of our business.

THE FINANCIAL BOTTOM LINE

Every business exists to make a profit. As stated in the first chapter, one of our company's objectives is "to grow profitably." Profit is critical to business success and growth.

> *"God and business do mix, and profit is a standard for determining the effectiveness of our combined efforts."*
> —C. WILLIAM POLLARD, *THE SOUL OF THE FIRM*

I am not a dreamy-eyed idealist. I am a realist and a capitalist, who surrounds himself with men and women who are also realists and capitalists. We know that we live by the laws of economics and the marketplace, and if we don't perform well financially and for our customers, we will go out of business and thousands of people will be without jobs. This is the reality of the global marketplace for every business today, whether the business is in manufacturing, high-tech software, or providing a service. We must have a solid financial bottom line. Therefore, we routinely set financial goals and do our utmost to achieve and exceed them, seeking to give our shareholders and stakeholders a good return on their investment.

In many ways, the financial goals we set for ourselves are the most easily defined and measured bottom-line goals. But for us, there is more to consider. Money is not the only reason for our company's existence. The financial bottom line is only one of three performance metrics we evaluate.

THE SOCIAL BOTTOM LINE

We want the values that guide our company to also guide the attitudes, behaviors, and decision making of our Factory Family Members both at work and at home. We believe our company's values can influence the whole of a person's life, including their families and the communities in which they live.

The integral connection between business and people was revealed in a negative way by the Enron case several years ago. Through the reckless and negligent actions of a few Enron executives, countless employees' lives were impacted, as well as the lives of those in their communities. Therefore, recognizing the ripple effect of our actions, we intentionally and consciously want our business to have a *positive* impact on the *whole* of every Factory Family Member, customer, supplier, and member of the community in which we conduct our business.

We are fully aware that every employee has a life "outside" CARDONE, even though some people may spend more awake time at work than they do at home. The influence of the workplace on an employee's overall life is difficult to measure, but it is important to us. If we can help people develop the whole of their life, those people will not only be happier and more fulfilled "inside" CARDONE, but they will be happier and more fulfilled "outside" the workplace as well. For this reason, our at-work values are our everywhere-else values too. They are to be seamlessly integrated into every facet of our lives.

Not long ago, one of our Family Factory Members, Albert, made this clear to me. Albert witnessed one of life's harshest realities. When he was only nine years old, he saw his mother murdered by his stepfather. As time passed, Albert got caught up in a repeated and vicious cycle of homelessness and prison. If things hadn't changed for him, there's little doubt he would have been just one more statistic reported in the newspaper.

In 2001, Albert came to CARDONE seeking a job, but he found a career. During his lunch hours he began to learn how to use the measuring instruments in our Engineering Department. His great attitude as an employee, outstanding attendance record, productivity, and willingness to learn soon got him promoted from the assembly line to leadership development. He became a successful Department Leader and is currently a manufacturing engineer. Albert said, "CARDONE not only gave me an opportunity to work, but an opportunity to live."

An opportunity to live! What a wonderful thing for a person to experience, and what a great thing for a business to promote.

People who feel valued in the workplace express their feelings in very practical ways, including increased loyalty and higher morale. They enjoy coming to work and go home with a sense of fulfillment. They recommend their place of employment to others. The net result is a "family" feeling within our business.

THE SPIRITUAL BOTTOM LINE

Although an individual may not claim a religion or profess faith in God, we believe every person is a "spiritual" being. Therefore, within the framework of good business practices, we give opportunities for people to express their beliefs in ways that are personally fulfilling, beneficial, and in keeping with our overall corporate values and principles. While we do not force our faith on our employees, we encourage our people to bring their faith to work.

> *"Values are the nonnegotiable principles that define character in a leader. Fewer than ten percent of organizations around the world have clear, written values. But values are important because they drive the behavior of people who work on your purpose and picture of the future."*
>
> —Ken Blanchard

These business practices are our way of recognizing people as spiritual beings. We encourage our employees to become their "highest and best" by developing spiritually, because we have found when people integrate their faith with their work, it translates into a higher quality of work, productivity, creativity, and a greater sense of personal significance.

INTERRELATED BOTTOM-LINE RESULTS

Do the factors related to the social bottom line and the spiritual bottom line impact the financial bottom line? Like many other businesses today, we are finding that they do.

The Home Depot places a premium on behaviors, feelings, experiences, and the work environment of its employees. Executives at Home Depot believe their corporate culture not only yields satisfied and fully engaged workers, but also impacts the financial bottom line in tangible ways. Their line of reasoning is this: satisfied and fully engaged workers treat customers differently, which results in a more satisfied and loyal customer base. The greater and more loyal the customer base the greater the opportunity for sales, and with increased sales come increased profits.

We have found at CARDONE that when people's behaviors are guided by values, positive energy permeates the workplace and the lines soften between management and worker. Regardless of their positions, employees feel a sense of ownership and take pride in the company. As a result, they are far more likely to develop a greater "managerial attitude" toward their own attitudes, efforts, and output. This is in direct keeping with a position Peter Drucker advocated years ago. He wrote,

> The demands for a "managerial attitude" on the part of even the lowliest worker is an *innovation*.
>
> No part of the productive resources of industry operates at a lower efficiency than the human resources. The few enterprises that have been able to tap this unused reservoir of human ability and attitude have achieved spectacular increases in productivity and output.
>
> In the better use of human resources lies the major opportunity for increasing productivity in the great majority of enterprises—so that the management of people should be the first and foremost concern of

> operating managements, rather than the management of things and techniques, on which attention has been focused so far.
>
> We also know what makes for the efficiency and productivity of the human resource of production. It is not primarily skill or pay; it is, first and foremost, an attitude—the one we call the "managerial attitude." By this we mean an attitude that makes the individual see his job, his work, and his product the way a manager sees them.[1]

Drucker maintained that an effective leader could potentially improve the productivity of his employees by more than 50 percent.

I have found people want to be part of a strong values-centered culture. Those who work from a foundation of values related to the whole person are high performers and pursue excellence in all they do. They display greater productivity and efficiency and produce maximum quality. They become the employees that every employer wants!

There are additional specific benefits to the company. At CARDONE we have seen:

- Lower turnover rates
- Fewer work-site injuries
- Lower absentee and tardy rates
- Improved ability to attract and retain talented people
- High levels of quality
- Increased productivity
- Improved morale

THE RIGHT BALANCE

There is a dynamic tension that exists in balancing the three bottom lines. In many ways, it would be less complicated to focus only on a financial bottom line. Our work, however, would not be as purposeful, rewarding, or effective.

There is no perfect balance or solution to balancing the three bottom lines. The balance you might strike among these three factors may be different from ours. I make no claims that we have the best balance or even the right balance. On the other hand, what we have works well for us. We consider the challenge in establishing the triple bottom line to have contributed to our overall business success and continued growth since 1970.

QUESTIONS ONLY YOU CAN ANSWER

1. What does the phrase "bottom line" mean to you in your professional and personal life?
2. Is profit the only thing that drives you and/or your business?
3. In what ways do you address the people in your company as "whole" people with financial, social, and spiritual facets?

3

Give Your Business to God

Giving Your Business or Career to God Is the First Step in Making Your Work Your Ministry

More than twenty years ago, we had a speaker in one of our early-morning, before-work chapel meetings. Our guest speaker for the day brought a friend with him. Following the chapel meeting, we gave both of them a tour of CARDONE. The friend of our speaker said, "I want to honor God in my business. Give me some of your thoughts."

"The first thing you have to do is give your business to God," I said. My guest gave me a blank stare. In that moment I realized before a person can give his business to God, he must first give his *life* to God. There's a big difference between just giving your "heart" and spiritual self to God and giving your entire "life" to God.

GIVING IT ALL

When I was in my first year in college I came to an important crossroads. At that point in my life, I had invited Christ into my life as my Savior, but I had not given Him all the parts of my life.

I am the kind of person who has always wanted to get the

most out of life. As a young person, I pursued life with a passion. Raised in a strict evangelical home, all the "don'ts" I heard in church became my goals! If the church said, "Don't do ______" . . . well, that was the very thing I decided I wanted to *do*. If the church said, "Don't smoke!" I smoked. When the church said, "No drinking!" I tried a little of that too.

I graduated fifty-ninth out of sixty students in my high school class. Actually, before graduation, number sixty dropped out of school to join the Marines. My academic record was not the result of a lack of effort or intellect. Thirty years after high school graduation, I discovered my poor performance in elementary schools and high school was related to an undetected learning disability.

Following high school, I tried to get into Syracuse University on a gymnastics scholarship, but my grades were too low. At that time, my father was on the founding Board of Regents at Oral Roberts University. Although I wasn't the least bit interested in attending a Christian college, I agreed to go to ORU for a semester, thinking I might be able to bring up my grades. Then, I could reapply and transfer to Syracuse. But mostly, I just wanted to get out of Philadelphia and be on my own. I wanted life on my terms.

> *"I think Christians in the workplace often fall into the trap that says, 'to really be a Christian, I have to leave the workplace and go to the mission field.' And yet there is no better mission field than right here in American industry."*
>
> —MATTHEW K. ROSE, PRESIDENT, CEO AND DIRECTOR, BURLINGTON NORTHERN SANTA FE CORPORATION

When I got to Oral Roberts University, two things surprised me. First, I thought I'd meet only "do's" and "don'ts" people at ORU. To my surprise, the students and faculty looked sharp and everyone seemed to have their lives together. I couldn't understand it. This was supposed to be a "religious" school. The more together the other students seemed to be, the more miserable I became.

The second surprise was that when I got away from the parental and teacher pressure, I found myself wanting to study harder and work on my grades. *I wanted* to work hard and make good grades. A good part of my motivation to improve my scholastic standing was so I could transfer to a secular school.

Though I worked hard, putting in long hours of study, at the end of the first semester, I had a 2.2 grade-point average. That was barely good enough to keep me in school, but it was not high enough for me to transfer to Syracuse. I was already discouraged and became even more discouraged. Everything I tried to do to improve my grade-point average failed. At the time, I didn't know I had a learning disability known as Attention Deficit Disorder (ADD). All I knew for sure was time after time, I studied and felt like I knew the information presented to me in class, but I never did well on the exams.

One evening, while I was studying in my dorm room, the feeling of failure pressed in on me like a blanket. Looking up from my desk and toward the bookshelf next to my bed, I saw my dusty Bible lying there. A thought hit me. Though I had been reared in a Christian home, went to Sunday school and knew a lot of Bible stories, I had never read the Bible with the purpose of trying to hear God speak to me. At that moment, I told myself I was going to read the Bible one last time, but "if there's nothing in it for me, then God has no place in my life journey."

I began reading the New Testament. Before I could get through the Gospel of Matthew, God spoke in my heart. He said, "Michael, you gave Me your heart, but you never gave Me your life. Give Me your life, and I will make a success out of you."

God did not speak to me in an audible voice, but I distinctly felt God asking me to give more of my time to Him and to give my time in service to others. It was part of a principle called "seed faith," which I was beginning to understand while at Oral Roberts University. In the Bible Jesus said, "Give, and it will be given to you . . ." (Luke 6:38). Through that verse God began to speak to me. I had a strong impression I was to get involved in the campus Christian Service Council. Since I needed every hour I could find for study, that didn't make sense to me, but I sensed God saying, "If you'll give some of your time to help other people, I will honor that offering and I will help you do better academically." So, that's what I did.

The university's Christian Service Council put me in touch with a twelve-year-old boy named Danny. Due to a terrible home life, Danny was living in an orphanage. As his assigned "big brother," I took him fishing, roller-skating, and helped him with his studies.

In the beginning I wasn't sure I had the ability to help him. Though spending time with Danny took time away from my own studies, the better I got to know this little guy with dusty blond hair and big blue eyes, the more convinced I became that spending time with him was the right thing for me to do. Danny was the person into whose life I was supposed to "plant" a seed of my time.

At first, Danny was suspicious. When I showed up the first day to take him fishing, he stared up at me and asked, "Why are you coming here?" All I could say was, "The Lord sent me." When he finally learned that I really wanted to be his friend, we had a great time together.

In addition to doing big-brother activities, I also invited Danny to pray with me. We thanked God for His gift of fun! Praying seemed to be new to Danny, but he took to it naturally. During the year I was his big brother, I began to notice I was becoming a positive influence in his life. Danny's home life eventually improved and he went back to live with his mother.

When We Edge God Out . . .

Ken Blanchard and Phil Hodges ask the question, "What is your leadership ego?" In 1923, Sigmund Freud defined *ego* as self-awareness. Blanchard and Hodges speak of *ego* as "edging God out" or "exalting God only." How is it that we edge out God in our business, workplace, or out of our lives? We do this when we:

- Trust in something other than God for our security
- Rely on sources other than God for our sufficiency
- Allow personal ego to get in the way
- Turn to others as our major supplier of self-worth
- Lose sight of God's unconditional love and become fearful of God, and eventually, fearful of others

"How might a person keep God at the center of his or her work life? Do just the opposite! Trust God first and foremost for your security, sufficiency, self-worth, confidence, and source of value, knowing that He is the Source of all creativity and opportunity."[1]
—Ken Blanchard and Phil Hodges, *The Servant Leader*

While I was spending time with Danny, an amazing thing happened to me. Just as God had impressed me to give my time as a "seed" to help someone else, God helped me discover a new method for studying and it worked for me! For some time I had been in the practice of taking copious notes in class. One night, while I was preparing to study for an exam, I felt a sudden urgency to *recopy* my notes. While doing this, I made an amazing discovery! The recopying process slowed my mind down so the information could really sink into my brain and the result was I found a way around my learning disability. In recent years I have learned this method of learning is frequently recommended to people with Attention Deficit Disorder. At that time, however, no professor or counselor had suggested this to me. People with ADD have a mind that simply cannot slow down. Their thoughts almost seem to tumble over one another seeking expression. But, when they recopy the text, their thoughts are forced to slow down so conceptual connections can be made in the brain. In the process students really *learn* the material they are recopying.

I began using this method of study for all my subjects and my grades soared. Eventually, I got involved in student government, made the Dean's List, and was listed in *Who's Who in American Colleges and Universities* when I graduated!

There is a greater lesson I learned. If I will turn everything over to God and trust Him, He will show me what to do. It was then that my father's favorite Bible verse became real to me: "Trust in the LORD with all your heart, and lean not on your own understanding; in all your ways acknowledge Him, and He shall direct your paths" (Proverbs 3:5–6). By everything, I mean *everything*. I not only gave my life to God, but I gave Him my relationships, ambitions, goals, and eventually my family, work, career, and company.

In my earlier years, I viewed myself as a loser. I had struggled all my life with school. I just didn't seem to be hearing the same drummer other kids heard. I was born with partial facial paralysis, which contributed to my low self-esteem. I couldn't imagine finding someone who would love me for who I was. But how could I expect someone to love me for who I was when I didn't even love myself?

As I gave my life completely to God, I began to recognize that God loved me, accepted me, and actually *created* me the way I am for a purpose. I finally realized God had given me my style of learning, my gifts, and physical attributes with His purposes in mind. The more I accepted these truths, the more I began to value myself. As my spiritual life transformed, my thinking changed. That is when my academic and social life began to improve too.

Looking back, I can hardly believe the life God has given me, and all the things He has enabled me to accomplish. Today, I am considered a leader in our industry. Even though I only have an undergraduate business degree, I am the CEO of Pennsylvania's largest privately owned manufacturer, with more than five thousand employees. I have a beautiful, loving wife, who has worked with me and stood by me faithfully for forty years. We have a loving family with three wonderful children and their spouses, each of whom is talented and productive in his or her chosen walk of life.

Through my experiences and the knowledge I have gained in life, I am convinced:

- Every person created by God has a purpose.
- Every person has been created to be a success.
- Real success is finding God's purpose for one's life.

These truths have been confirmed to me on a number of occasions and through a number of different Bible verses, which include the following:

- "I can do all things *through Christ* who strengthens me" (Philippians 4:13, emphasis mine).
- "Not by might nor by power, but by My Spirit" (Zechariah 4:6).
- "But remember the LORD your God, for it is he who gives you the ability to produce wealth" (Deuteronomy 8:18 NIV).

A person who looks to the past for indicators about the future is like a mountain climber who looks down rather than up. The same is true for a person who trusts in his or her own resources for wisdom and creativity. There simply is no match between the latest management strategy and the wisdom God gives through the Bible. No current business fad can be as creative as the Creator of all things.

"RE-GIFT" YOURSELF

There is a term we sometimes use lightheartedly in our society about gifts we receive, but don't really need or want. We say we will "re-gift" someone. This means we will pass on the gift to someone else. The term *re-gift* is actually a serious concept! I believe God calls us to re-gift every gift He has given to us, including every talent we have received, the hours and days He gives us on this earth, and the money and resources He puts in our hands. By this, I mean we are to plant the gifts God has given to us in something that has the potential to grow, expand, or bless others. The Bible encourages this, saying, "He who sows sparingly will also reap sparingly, and he who sows bountifully will also reap bountifully . . . for God loves a cheerful giver" (2 Corinthians 9:6–7). We are to plant our gifts and expect

God to give us a harvest and use it for good. Our responsibility is to give and do our best; God is responsible for the outcome. When we invest our gifts in others, our gifts grow. What better purpose is there than to grow our business and our profits, so we have more resources to "re-gift"?

If you give God your heart, your talents, and your life, He will do things in and through you that are beyond your imagination and expectations. His plan is better than any man-made plan. He sees the whole picture and knows the best plan for you to experience the ultimate happiness, fulfillment, and significance you desire. He will multiply you according to His ultimate plan, which includes His plan for your life and the lives of those around you.

That doesn't mean you won't have problems or struggles in your life. But it does mean you won't have to face those struggles alone. You will have Someone guiding and helping you.

Is there something keeping you from "giving it all" to God? If so, I strongly encourage you to face and overcome that hurdle today. You will be amazed at what God can and will do in your life, business, and career when you give *all* to Him.

QUESTIONS ONLY YOU CAN ANSWER

1. Have you given your business—your career—to God?
2. Have you given all of your *life* to God?
3. In what ways are you seeking to *re-gift* yourself?

4

The Ministry of Business

There Are Many Types of Mission Fields . . . Including Businesses

Through the years, I have encountered a number of young people who are trying to decide what to do with their lives. Some seek the advice of a teacher, mentor, guidance counselor, or some other trusted person. My hope for them is that they do not receive the same kind of advice that well-meaning people gave me when I was seeking guidance about God's purpose for my life. The way my early-life "advisors" saw it, to make a difference you had to be in some sort of church ministry. With good intentions, a number of people told me I should become a pastor. Others suggested I go overseas as a missionary, work for a Christian organization, or devote my life to the Peace Corps or some other good cause.

To some degree, I followed their advice. But it turned out to be a very frustrating experience for me and for those I was attempting to help.

No one told me that I should consider using my God-given talents to do the one thing my father hoped I would do: work alongside him to build a successful and unique business, and eventually assume the leadership of that company. No one seemed to consider that particular career path to be sufficiently significant or spiritual.

I thought, prayed, and reflected on my past. In the end, I came to the conclusion that I *wanted* to accept my father's invitation to start a business with him after I graduated from college. Once I made that decision, I have never doubted it was the right decision and God's plan for my life.

One of the things I've discovered is when you are fully using the unique abilities God has built into you, you will feel a tremendous sense of joy, fulfillment, and satisfaction. There are many days when I feel just a little guilty about calling my work a "job." I enjoy my work so much that it doesn't seem like work. I absolutely love what I do. I get up early in the morning and can't wait to begin using my God-given creativity and to discover my potential and all the learning opportunities God has planned for me in the day ahead. Knowing I can tap into the greatest Source of creativity in the universe both energizes and amazes me.

> *"Do not let your occupation block your destiny; instead, allow your destiny to shape your business by turning it into your ministry."*
> —Ed Silvoso, Anointed for Business

I find tremendous satisfaction in seamlessly living out my beliefs and values from home to work by creating things that are well made, meeting customer's needs and helping others develop their potential. Rarely do I express my beliefs by *talking* about them. Instead, I choose to express my beliefs on a daily basis through my creativity, through my actions, and by *producing* something of value. I believe people *see* the message of our lives more than they hear our words. What I have discovered is I have a ministry of business.

HOW I CAME TO SEE BUSINESS AS MY MINISTRY

Like a number of other Christian young people, I thought giving my life to God meant He would immediately send me to some third-world country. I didn't know then what I know now: God doesn't want any miserable missionaries. He doesn't force us to do things we are not suited to do. When He calls us to go somewhere and to do something, He gives us the gifts and abilities we need to fulfill that calling. Our Creator knows our personalities and giftedness. When we're doing what He created us to do, we will find fulfillment in it. That's certainly been my experience.

During my sophomore year in college, I went with a group of other students to Fort Lauderdale, Florida, for spring break. Our goal was to share our faith in God with other college students.

Fort Lauderdale was known as *the* place to party over spring break and only a few of the young people there were interested in hearing what we had to say. I felt awkward trying to talk to them about my faith when they were hungover. After a while, I became more direct and I found myself becoming angry with the kids on the beach who refused to listen or seemed disinterested. My direct approach made many of them angry. At the end of the week, I left with the feeling that my witnessing efforts at the beach were a disaster and I was a failure.

I had gone on this trip with the intention of discerning whether God was directing me into full-time religious work of some type. The answer came back . . . obviously not. Deep inside I knew this was *not* what I was created to do. In knowing what I was *not* to do, I started asking God what He had created me to do.

Before I could fully embrace what I believed was God's call to have a ministry in business, I had to come to this understanding:

I have been designed as a one-of-a-kind person with a divine purpose on this earth.

Over time, I have come to understand that God created me with a contrarian's perspective. I tend to look for another way of doing things. In business I wanted to be a positive influence and provide leadership in a place that didn't have enough positive words. I wanted to model faith-based values and show by my *life* that Biblical principles work in today's world.

For me, the place where I discovered I could make the greatest impact was in business. Business gave me the opportunity to model my beliefs and values in a different way and to different people.

BUSINESS AS A SACRED CALLING

My father, Michael Cardone Sr., was part of a church where the prevailing understanding seemed to be that a "deeply committed" Christian needed to work in a full-time clergy or ministry position. Being a deeply committed Christian, my father attended Bible school for a while to prepare for full-time religious work, but then realized that he was not a good public speaker and wasn't likely to become one. He turned to a career in business, which is where both his heart and skills found fulfillment.

It wasn't until a number of years later, however, that a minister said to my father:

> Millions of people don't go to church or attend any kind of religious services or activities. In order

> to reach as many people as possible, God needs to have people working as businessmen, as dentists and doctors, as actors in Hollywood, and in all other fields of art, professional service, commerce, and industry. Those who are committed Christians in these areas also have a sacred call of God on their lives to display the gospel by what they *do*. Their sermons are in their actions and words on the job, not in a pulpit.

That message took deep root in my father and he never again questioned whether he was doing God's work by building great companies. He had found a *ministry of business* that he loved.

EVERY PERSON IS A UNIQUE CREATION WITH UNIQUE PURPOSE

While I was a student at Oral Roberts University, I heard a message by its founder and evangelist, Oral Roberts, about an incident in the life of Jesus. That sermon greatly impacted my life. Here is a summary of the story (see Luke 5:1–6).

> Jesus was standing near a lake, surrounded by a crowd of people who were pressing toward Him to hear His teaching. He stepped into a boat belonging to a fisherman named Simon, and then asked Simon to pull away from the shore so He could continue teaching from this

> floating platform. Everyone could see Jesus and hear Him better if He was in the boat than if He stayed on the shore.
>
> After Jesus finished His message, He instructed Simon to go out farther into the lake and let down his fishing nets for a catch. Simon and his crew had already fished all night—which was the ideal time for fishing on that lake—and they had caught no fish. Nevertheless, Simon did what Jesus said and he caught so many fish that his nets began to break. He called upon other fishermen to join him in the biggest catch of their lives.

As I heard this sermon I was hit with the understanding that Simon's boat was his *business*. Simon made a living as a fisherman using that boat. Jesus asked Simon to give Him his single biggest asset for a higher purpose. In this real-life story, Jesus was trying to show Simon what happens when a person lets go of something completely and gives it to God. When we surrender our business to God, He can do more *through the person who has surrendered* than anything that person could ever do on his own. I began to think to myself, *if God could produce incredible results with a professional fisherman and his boat and nets, what might He do if I gave him my life and my business?* Giving my life to God meant that I was willing to be the person God created me to be. In the end, that was the best, most natural, and easiest thing I could do. It took all the pressure off of me. It put me in the position to be a success on God's terms, which has been far more rewarding than anything I ever could have imagined. It put me in a position for significance, fulfillment, and deep satisfaction in life.

Does giving one's assets to God mean God will make that person rich financially? Not necessarily, since there are many practical, human decisions that contribute to financial success.

Does financial success make us happier? Not necessarily. We all know rich and financially successful people who are miserable.

Does God create us for failure or for success? I believe strongly He created us for success, but success includes far more than financial wealth. Giving our assets to God means that God will make us *more* than rich financially. When we give our lives to Him, He puts us on the path for our highest and best success, a life that accomplishes more than we could do or achieve on our own. True success in life is overflowing with purpose and significance. Financial success may or may not be a part of that.

I have no doubt that God uses our *resources* and our work at CARDONE, including our manufacturing plants, our equipment, our processes, and our products to help bring about and fulfill His purposes. Those purposes are not just financial.

Simon is a great example of what can be accomplished when a person gives his business to God. Only when he gave up his professional pride and was willing to listen did Jesus produce amazing results.

After Simon caught this miracle boatload of fish, Jesus called Simon to become a "fisher of men." He asked Simon to leave his boat and become one of His disciples (see Luke 5:10 and Matthew 4:18–20). Simon wanted to be a fisherman, but God created him to be a change agent in the world. That role was much more than Simon could fathom or achieve on his own. For years, this part of the sermon troubled me, because I thought it meant God wanted me to leave my business in order to follow and serve Him.

My earlier experience in Fort Lauderdale helped me realize

God wasn't calling me to *leave* my business, but rather he was calling me to *turn* my business into a place where I would have a genuine ministry. Simon needed to leave his boat and follow Jesus in order to learn how to best impact people's lives. But God's plan for me was to keep using my boat (business) as a means for ministering to others. I'm not Simon Peter and Simon Peter wasn't Michael Cardone Jr. God has a unique plan for each unique person.

I like the way Tom Chappell, cofounder and CEO of Tom's of Maine, has described the process of finding his place in life in his book *Managing Upside Down*. After his company began to achieve great success, Chappell went to talk to his pastor and the pastor's wife. "I think that I would like to study more about theology," he said. "I'm not really understanding my mission in life."

His pastor's wife challenged him, "How do you know that Tom's of Maine isn't your ministry?"

After that meeting Chappell concluded, "Maybe my business was my mission in life. The idea of finding—through my business—a higher mission than making money was not the clean, crisp solution I had thought I was looking for." [1]

THE DAY I KNEW I WAS IN "MINISTRY"

While I was a student at Oral Roberts University, I heard Oral Roberts make two statements repeatedly. These two statements took deep root in my heart. They challenged me as a young person and continue to challenge me today.

The first statement was a challenge to "go into every man's world."

The second statement was a mandate Oral Roberts said he heard from God about those of us who would become alumni of ORU: "Raise up your students to hear My voice, to go where My light is seen dim, My voice is heard small, and My healing power is not known—even to the uttermost bounds of the earth. Their work will exceed yours, and in this I am well-pleased." What I encountered in the process of God turning my life from failure to success has become my passion to share with others. *I believe God can turn other peoples' lives from failure to success.*

> *"But seek first the kingdom of God and His righteousness, and all these things shall be added to you."*
>
> —Matthew 6:33

Although I readily adopted in my heart the two concepts Oral Roberts shared, the first time I saw evidence of these concepts at *work* in my life came through a personal encounter I had with an employee named Felipo. It occurred early in my career at CARDONE Industries.

Felipo was a middle-aged man who had come up the hard way. He was the tough, macho type, who had little use for college guys. He spoke broken English and had a rough personality. I, in turn, had little patience with what I perceived to be his proud, bull-headed attitude.

Then, one day a problem arose with a power-steering pump. The rotor on the cam assembly was not working as it was designed to work, causing a whining noise when we tested it. I tried to isolate the problem, but couldn't identify it. Felipo came along and offered to help. At first I wanted to shrug him away. Then I remembered, "God shows no partiality," and I knew I needed to show respect to Felipo and accept his offer of help. After I explained the problem to Felipo, he picked up the power-steering pump, looked at it, felt inside the cylinder, and said, "Michael, something seems to be a little rough on the inside where the cam wears."

I took a closer look. Sure enough, I could see a small spot worn by the cam. Once the problem was clearly identified, we were able to solve it quickly.

In the course of getting better acquainted with Felipo, I realized he and the others with whom I worked were the people I could positively influence. Over time I was able to help Felipo with some of the things that were a "little rough" in his life and the lives of his family members. This epiphany was *the* moment in which I felt I was, indeed, involved in the ministry of business. As I befriended and worked with Felipo, I realized this is where I was to positively influence people.

For me, the place where God's voice is often heard small, His light is seen dim, and His power is not known is the world of business. Through the decades I have encountered literally hundreds of men and women who faced enormous challenges in their lives, and who were facing those challenges without God. They did not hear God's voice. They did not see His light or know His power.

Every time I can help people find their purpose and help them understand God wants to do meaningful things in their lives more wonderful than they can possibly imagine, things that will give them genuine satisfaction and significance, then, I know, without a shadow of doubt, I am involved in *ministry*. It is not about me. It's about the other people and about the great things God has in store for them.

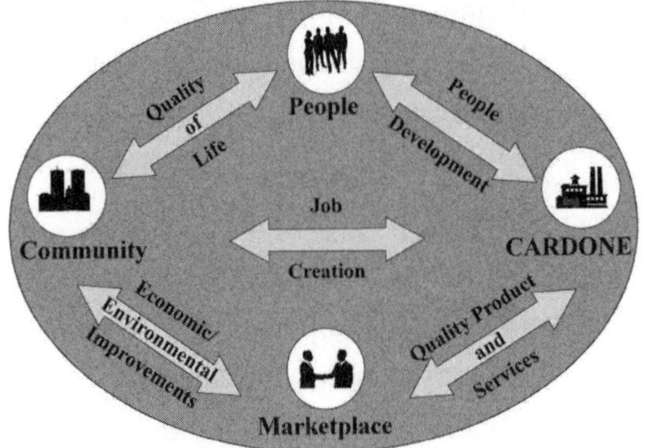

The ministry of business is the impact a business has on its employees, their families, and the community, while at the same time meeting and exceeding the demands of the marketplace.

QUESTIONS ONLY YOU CAN ANSWER

1. Do you know the unique purpose for which God created you?
2. Do you see your business or career as a place of ministry? Why or why not?
3. In what ways might your business or career become your place of ministry?

5

In Pursuit of Excellence

There's No Substitute for Being the Best

I don't desire to be in a spotlight, receiving awards. In my opinion, awards are just what they are—wooden plaques, paper certificates, and other objects. However, if I am given the opportunity to rally support for the things in which I truly believe, then I am willing to step into a spotlight. Such an opportunity came in 2005, when I was asked to serve as chairman of the Motor & Equipment Manufacturers Association (MEMA), the major industry trade group for nearly eight hundred companies in the auto parts industry. These companies have aggregate sales of approximately $500 billion.

If you aren't familiar with MEMA, you may not realize what a radical invitation this was. I was the first executive from the remanufacturing industry to fill this post in the association's 102-year history. Before that year, all chairmen had come from the ranks of new original equipment parts manufacturers, with the overwhelming majority of them from publicly held companies.

I was honored to serve as MEMA chairman and I believe my selection illustrates the power of values. There are few remanufacturers in MEMA. While we are one of the largest remanufacturers in the world, the multinational, publicly held MEMA members dwarf our size. What is known about us in the marketplace is how we operate, produce products, perform for our customers, and treat people. People in our industry know CARDONE as a values-driven company. They also know I am a tireless promoter of three values: quality, performance, and integrity. These three values are what I consider to be the pillars of excellence.

WHO SEES WHAT CAN'T BE SEEN?

A *real* commitment to quality is expecting quality even for those things that cannot be seen.

Phidias, the greatest sculptor of ancient Greece, around 440 BC made the statues that to this day—2,400 years later—still stand on the roof of the Parthenon in Athens. But when Phidias submitted his bill, the city accountant of Athens refused to pay it.

"These statues stand on the roof of the temple, and on the highest hill in Athens," he said. "Nobody can see anything but their fronts. Yet, you have charged us for sculpturing them in the round, that is, for doing their backsides, which nobody can see."

"You are wrong," Phidias retorted. "The gods can see them."[1]

—Peter Drucker, *The Daily Drucker*

My father used to say often, "Excellence in all things and all to the glory of God." It is the pursuit of excellence that drives us because that is a worthy goal in life. I believe in doing things well and striving to be the best, knowing God inspires and enables excellence. It is He who compels us to strive for quality, performance, and integrity.

Many may question whether or not a business in today's global market can be successful using biblical principles and the leadership model of Jesus Christ. I am convinced it can.

People in countless professions pursue excellence and strive for it unceasingly. A physician's goal is total excellence, not "acceptable quality." Would you accept a physician saying his goal is "six sigma," a six-out-of-a-million error rate, the highest quality standard in manufacturing? Of course, not! Every patient wants a physician who will perform a procedure and operate flawlessly 100 percent of the time! In like manner, I want to be among those who not only strive for excellence, but a business that succeeds in delivering our products and services without error. We pursue excellence, because our customers expect perfect products and services.

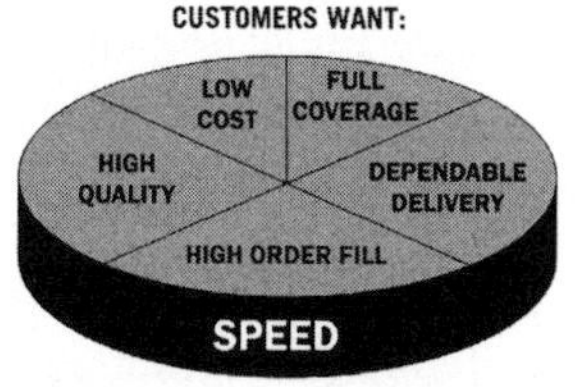

We have defined excellence as what our customers look for in a supplier. It includes high-quality products and services, high levels of order fill, full coverage on all makes and models, dependable delivery, and low competitive prices. All of these working together embody what we call "The CARDONE Circle of Excellence." In addition to excellent performance we must respond and perform with urgency-speed.[2]

Honoring God is about performing with excellence and being the best you can be. Performing with excellence gives us the best opportunity to have a positive influence. That is why pursuing excellence is part of our culture. It is who we are. That's why our mission statement at CARDONE is aimed squarely at being the best.

Our Mission Statement
To Be the Best Remanufacturer in the World

NO SUBSTITUTE FOR QUALITY PERFORMANCE

Quality is a given in today's global business environment. You must have quality products and services to survive. Our relentless pursuit of quality is perhaps the foremost factor that enables our company to compete on a global scale and with other larger corporations.

Following an accident in 1983, my father's commitment to quality became even more obvious to me. A trucking company's tractor-trailer loaded with CARDONE products was carrying a load to one of our customers, when an accident caused the tractor-trailer to tip over on the highway. As soon as we received word of the accident, we packed and shipped a duplicate order to our customer that same day and sent a crew out to help retrieve the cargo. All of the products that were retrieved were unpacked and put through the entire remanufacturing process all over again to make certain that each one was fully functional.

"Success is peace of mind which is a direct result of self-satisfaction in knowing you did your best to become the best that you are capable of becoming."
—Coach John Wooden, *Coach John Wooden's Pyramid of Success*

Since the packaging was hardly damaged, someone asked why we hadn't simply loaded these boxes onto another truck to send them on. "We couldn't take that chance," my father said. "Even though our customer may not have known the car parts had been through an accident, we knew it and God knew it. The only way we could be certain each part was *perfect* was if we remanufactured and tested each one."

When it comes to quality assurance, one of the questions we ask ourselves is, "Would I put the part I am making on my family car?" Quality was important to my father and it is important to me today, because when a customer opens our box, we know he expects perfect parts from us.

Quality is the number-one priority of professional automotive technicians that repair our vehicles and keep them on the road. The professional technician knows his reputation and the potential for repeat business depends on satisfied customers. The parts installed must function perfectly. Although we do not promote our brand on the hood of a race car or through consumer advertising, we rank as one of the most recognized brands in the industry. Our pursuit of excellence in all things has resulted in a reputation for being the best. For years, CARDONE products, under various brand labels, have been ranked number one. Two hundred twenty aftermarket customers participated in Great Lakes Marketing's latest customer satisfaction survey. Nine major suppliers were identified. The survey showed that CARDONE branded products were preferred over our next closest competitor by a ratio of 3 to 1, indicating that CARDONE is the supplier of choice in the automotive aftermarket.

"BEST" MEANS ZERO DEFECTS

Every industry has its own standards of quality. Our customers expect perfect parts every time. Their standard is zero defects and that's our standard as well. We look at quality this way: "We don't want to be good enough. We want to be the *best*." For us, best in quality means zero defects. That is our standard and it's what our customers and the industry have come to expect from us.

> *"Excellence is the spotlight on imperfection."*
> —Dom Foti, VP of CARDONE European Operations

When you are dealing with safety issues involving automotive products, only 100 percent reliability is acceptable. Therefore, having zero defects is the only acceptable standard.

Our quality statement of policy states:

> We believe the quality of our products and services is the most important issue to our customers: therefore, quality is the foundation of our corporate culture. We will produce products and services that meet customer requirements every time, on time. We will continually improve products and processes as the path to excellence.

Quality guru Philip Crosby teaches quality can be measured in objective financial terms and calculates that the price of nonconformance is 25 percent of operating costs in manufacturing and 40 percent in service companies. We also believe that every instance of *nonconformance*, the term for whatever does not meet customers' requirements, i.e., a defective part produced, unacceptable service provided, or inaccurate paperwork, *can* be prevented. We put as many preventive and corrective measures in place as necessary to ensure that no product leaves our factory with a defect and no service is provided without excellence.

Our Zero-Defects Policy goes as far back as 1934, when my father was working at Bonney's Garage. One evening, Harry, a salesman at the garage, handed Dad a blackened, greasy car part about as big as an apple. My father recognized it as a well-worn windshield wiper motor. Harry asked, "Do you think you can fix this?" My father studied the motor for a moment and replied, "If they manufactured it, then it can be remanufactured."

Harry next said, "Here's my idea. I visit a lot of garages and service stations. They all have lots of these defective wiper motors. They'd be happy for me to take them off their hands for nothing or for just a few pennies." Then, Harry proposed that the two of them rebuild those old wiper motors and resell them.

That evening my father went home and took apart the old wiper unit. He laid out all the individual parts and studied them. After determining how the motor worked, he searched for the part that seemed to be getting the most wear. It was easy for him to spot. It was the leather paddle, which, in responding to intermittent air pressure, actuated the wiper blades. He punched out the rivets holding the paddle, removed it, got a piece of stronger and better leather, made a new paddle, and riveted it back in. Then he cleaned and polished each part and reassembled the wiper motor. It looked brand new.

The next morning Dad was fully prepared to show Harry what he had done, but a nagging question kept him from doing so. "What will Harry think of me as a mechanic if this motor doesn't work when he puts it back on his car? How can I be certain it will work properly?"

Dad went to one of the cars in the garage and replaced its good wiper motor with his remanufactured motor, started the engine, switched the lever . . . and nothing happened. He removed the wiper motor and set it next to the good one on the table. Then he took both of them apart, comparing each component. This time he found a gasket that needed replacing. He replaced it and tried his test again. Still nothing. A third time he disassembled it and discovered dirt clogging the air inlet valve. He cleaned the valve and tested his rebuilt motor a third time. Success! He *knew* his unit worked and he could show it with a real sense of accomplishment to Harry. It was in that early business experience that my dad began to realize his name, family reputation, and future business depended upon the quality of the products he produced.

The remanufacturing of wiper motors provided a good part-time "extra" job for my father. As Harry brought more and more wiper motors to him, Dad set up an assembly line, of sorts, for remanufacturing them. From that experience my father developed the first assembly-line process for remanufacturing and it revolutionized the industry. Years later, my father was recognized as the pioneer of the remanufacturing industry and was inducted into the Automotive Hall of Fame alongside other industry icons, such as Henry Ford, Louis Chevrolet, Eiji Toyoda, Lee Iacocca, and others.

Since testing is expensive, some companies do what they call "representative" or "statistical" testing. By testing only a percentage of their products, they lower their costs. No such hit-and-miss approaches were ever good enough for my father. He would say to me, "Our name is on the box. How do you want people to think about our family?" He also said, "Testing every part lets me sleep well at night. I don't know how I'd feel if an untested brake part we supplied, failed on a rain-slick road and caused a fatal accident." I couldn't agree more.

Having zero defects is the only acceptable standard for a business carrying our family name. Pursuing excellence keeps us on the right track to achieve our mission: "To Be the Best Remanufacturer in the World."

CARDONE Industries Quality Policy

- *We believe* the quality of our products and services is the most important issue to our customers: therefore, quality is the foundation of our corporate culture.
- *We will produce* products and services that meet customer requirements every time on time.
- *We will continually improve* products and processes as the path to excellence.

—Evan Curry, CARDONE Sr. VP of Quality and Compliance

QUESTIONS ONLY YOU CAN ANSWER

1. How do you as a consumer define quality?
2. How does your company define quality?
3. How does your company translate a concern for quality into performance standards?
4. How do you pursue excellence?

6

Creating a Business "Family"

Treating the Person Next to You in the Workplace As If He Is Next of Kin

Vicki came to work with us in 1989. She came from a war-torn nation in Africa and later told us, "I had big dreams. I wanted to get a good education, get a good job, and find Prince Charming." A few years later, her dreams had been dashed.

Her husband was in prison, leaving her to provide and care for their young children alone. When Vicki began working with us on the smog-pump assembly line, she was emotionally stressed out and miserable.

Vicki's team leader noted she was repeatedly late for work or absent. The leader addressed the issue with her and worked with Human Resources to see what else could be done. At CARDONE, we see repeated absenteeism and tardiness as problems that need to be explored, addressed, and resolved.

Our Human Resources Department and chaplains began to work with Vicki to address the practical causes for her absences. The counsel from our chaplain gave her encouragement with workable ideas, contacts, and possible solutions that would make Vicki's life manageable and, hopefully, would enable her to keep her job. Vicki's tardiness and absenteeism were directly related to the morning challenges she faced. Every workday, Vicki had to get her young children to daycare. Then, since she had no car, she frantically raced to catch two buses and two trains, which needed to operate "on time" in order for her to make the right connections and arrive at the factory on time.

We Value Our People

We are committed to the following:

- Every person has intrinsic value and worth.
- Every person has a unique contribution to make to the company.
- All people are treated equally with dignity.
- An individual's family needs will be given priority.

—Frank Zgrablich, CARDONE Executive VP of HR

After many conversations with one of our chaplains, Vicki began to turn things around in her life. She turned to God and experienced a tremendous renewal through the hope that God could help her rise above her difficulties. Vicki made the changes needed to simplify her life, help her children, and reduce her travel time. This enabled her to refocus her efforts at work and her work performance improved. She soon was promoted to a better-paying job as part of our maintenance staff. Her increased salary was enough to help her buy a small house closer to the factory.

Over time, Vicki's life became more stable and she began to

make even bigger plans for her future. She started attending classes at a nearby school of ministry, and eventually, she earned a degree in biblical theology. On the job, she took full advantage of our employee-training improvement program. She spent her lunch hours on the company computers, practicing typing skills, and learning various computer programs.

In the late 1990s, ten years after she began working with us, she took a skills test and passed it with flying colors. She was promoted to an office position, where she has continued to advance. Her life has so changed that she now goes by her proper name, Victoria.

At home, Victoria was reunited with her husband. Two of her children are in college and one is married with children. She is very active in her church as a Sunday school teacher and leader of a women's ministry.

Victoria is not an isolated example. Through the years, we have seen many of our Factory Family Members, sometimes out of desperation, take the biblical principles that we use in our business, such as quality, integrity, and excellence, and apply them to their personal lives. It's very rewarding to see these individuals growing and improving professionally *and* personally.

As you can see, we did not treat Victoria like an "expendable employee." We treated her like family. Families have problems, but family members care for one another and are committed to helping each other work through their problems and conflicts. That's the approach we have taken in creating a Factory Family.

At the top of our list of core corporate values is this:

We Value Our People

The only way I know how to truly value those with whom we work is to have an attitude toward them that communicates, "You are family."

> *"We often consider ourselves to be many things to the people who work alongside us—coworkers, teammates, contributors, competitors—but we often forget to be the one thing that every person wants: a friend."*
>
> —John C. Maxwell, *The 21 Irrefutable Laws of Leadership*

A FUNCTIONAL, FAMILY PERSPECTIVE

What is it that makes a person *family* rather than *employee?* It is how we think and view our employees. That is why we call them Factory Family Members. We really care about them. Our people are our most important asset. We value them personally and call our employees *by name*. We expect our leaders to get to know, express interest in, and assist their people for professional and personal growth.

All leadership is committed to know as many of our Factory Family Members by name as is possible. With five thousand employees, that is a challenge. But, it is a challenge we consider to be important and one at which we work every day.

What is it that *you* desire for *your* family members? In all likelihood, you looking for these five things:

- Trust. You want to be able to count on your family members and you expect them to be trustworthy. Creating an environment of trust and truthfulness is key to a family culture.
- Engagement. You look for your family members to be fully involved and passionate in caring for the family.

- Development. You expect your family members to be supportive, encouraging one another to reach their full potential.
- Fulfillment. You desire the best for your family members. You want them to be satisfied, to be content, and to enjoy life.
- Recognition. You want your family members to be acknowledged for their contributions, achievements, and progress.

We pursue all five of these things for our employees at CARDONE and look for practical ways we can implement policies and programs to address each of these areas.

As a growing business, we expect those who work with us to do high-quality work, as productively and efficiently as possible. But, we also want for our employees what *they* want for themselves—a secure job where they can work and be valued as a person, have a sense of belonging, and be a part of something bigger than they are.

Each family member is called upon to:

- Respect all other Factory Family Members.
- Preserve the dignity of other Factory Family Members.
- Show loyalty to other Factory Family Members.
- Encourage other Factory Family Members.

In every family there is a certain amount of dysfunction, and part of the challenge of living in a family is working through that dysfunction until it is corrected. Not every person at CARDONE embraces the concept of being a "family member." Though we strive to create a family atmosphere, we don't always succeed in developing the same sense of family in each person who comes to work with us. But . . . we *want to.* We work toward creating an environment in which each new employee will take an active part in our Factory Family and work with us to achieve our goals of excellence, quality, and integrity. Our goal is for them to work *with* us, not merely *for* us.

> *"I would rather associate with a bunch of half-crazed people in the pursuit of perfection than bump along with a bunch of comfortable people who are in the process of disappearing and just don't know it."*
> —ROGER PENSKE, RACING CAR DRIVER AND TRACK OWNER

At times, some family members choose, by their own free will, to leave our company's family. While they are with CARDONE, we work with our employees as best as we know how to help them develop strong skills, self-value, and good performance. There are times, however, when either an employee feels they must leave for their purposes, or due to unresolved issues at work, a Factory Family Member's employment may be terminated by us. In those cases, we want to part with them in the best possible way, saying, "We wish you well. Go where you *can* succeed and where you can feel fully valued and fulfilled." We take pride in a Factory Family Member who has an opportunity to develop even further at another job or in another industry because of what they have learned and how they developed during their time at CARDONE.

TWO KEY "FAMILY" CONCERNS

There are two additional issues that are often left unaddressed by businesses. The first issue is anxiety and frustration. The second issue is stress. At CARDONE we are concerned about these two issues and concern is part of what helps to create the "family" feel to our corporate culture.

Every person has anxieties, worries, concerns, and frustrations. Many companies require employees to leave their problems at the front door as they enter the workplace. The truth is, they can't. People can't leave all their problems "at home."

As opportunities present themselves, I ask people who do *not* work for CARDONE how they feel about their jobs. Some tell me that they feel they are treated without personal regard. They feel their employers don't care in the least about their lives outside the workplace. Still others feel overt prejudice or some form of harassment at work. There are many ways that we address these issues at CARDONE, some of which are discussed later in this book.

It is our sincere goal that those who work with us feel as if we:

- Value them as whole human beings—spirit, mind, and body.
- Care about the totality of their lives—their marriages, families, and communities.
- Ensure they are safe emotionally and physically in the workplace.

An important key to caring is *listening*. To be effective, the listener must be trusted, caring, and be available to the employee. At CARDONE that listener might be a team leader, a chaplain, or another Factory Family Member.

We want to create an environment in which people can open up and express their ideas, concerns, and suggestions without fear.

And the only way to know a family member has deep concerns is to give that person the time and opportunity to express his or her concerns. We saw this need and developed the roles and responsibilities of our chaplains. The chaplains are in addition to union representatives, leadership, and human resources.

Concerning stress, one group of researchers developed a Stress Cost Formula to measure the cost of stress on organizations and individuals. In an article titled "Counting the Cost of Stress," Rebecca Goldin reported on how *stress* is the underlying factor for:

- 19 percent of the total cost of absenteeism
- 40 percent of total turnover cost
- 55 percent of the cost for employee assistance programs
- 30 percent of short-term and long-term disability costs
- 10 percent of drug-plan costs to cover psychotherapeutic care
- 60 percent of the total cost of workplace accidents[1]

I often work long hours in a day. Though I am busy, I am not stressed. In fact, I love those 3:00 a.m. bursts of creativity I often experience. The fact of the matter is I have to discipline myself to get sufficient sleep. My work schedule would be highly stressful, for most people. Also, if I were *forced* to work at a very slow pace with very few outlets for creativity, I *would* feel tremendous stress!

Ultimately, the person feeling stressed defines what is stressful to them. And, a person who is feeling stress will *show* their feelings in definite, and sometimes subtle, ways.

If you tour CARDONE, you will encounter a labor-intensive, highly efficient, and productive factory environment in which thousands of people are doing the work of remanufacturing auto parts. This involves disassembling, cleaning, repairing, assembling, testing, and packaging tens of thousands of auto parts every day. This work can be hard, hot, and noisy. Those who visit and tour our factory floors are amazed to find many of our workers smiling as they do this complex, demanding, high-performance work.

When we observe a Factory Family Member who is *not* smiling and doesn't have a positive word or a helpful attitude, it can be a sign something is troubling that individual. Rather than ignoring it, we intervene, demonstrate care, and look for ways we can help that person get back on track. Caring for our employees also requires us to have people who will act as our "eyes." Such a person may be a leader, a chaplain, or another Factory Family Member. All of our leaders are advised to observe, listen, and care enough to get involved in the lives of employees.

> *"The best minute I spend is the one I invest in people."*
> —KENNETH BLANCHARD, *THE ONE MINUTE MANAGER*

Because we regard our coworkers as Factory Family Members, we are concerned about what concerns them. When our coworkers feel our level of concern for them, they come to regard themselves as we regard them: *Family*.

PRACTICAL "FAMILY" EXPRESSIONS

There are various things we do at CARDONE to convey the way we feel about our Factory Family Members. This involves recognizing high performing Factory Family Members through the following awards:

Cornerstone Award celebrates the extraordinary character of Factory Family Members whose words and actions are the foundation of CARDONE's objectives and values. This award is our highest honor, because it recognizes not a single action but a career that shaped our business and corporate culture. This lifetime achievement award is the benchmark for all Factory Family Members to follow.

Presidential Citation is the highest award for excellence. It is awarded to Factory Family Members who go beyond their job requirements by pioneering a new program, system, process, or innovation. It is given to those making a significant impact on the development of our business, reengineering an area of business, and performing to the highest standards.

Gideon Award is a team award. It is given for exceptional team performance that exceeds goals, benefits customers, or cuts costs. In the Bible, Gideon was the leader of just 300 men and yet they defeated a much larger enemy, proving the power of teamwork.

The Michael Cardone Sr. Quality Award is given to Factory Family Members who embrace our quality management system, and as examples, they inspire others to strive for excellence in their work.

The Frances Cardone Women in the Industry Award is given to women in our business who have demonstrated excellence in their work and made special contributions to the automotive industry or to CARDONE Industries.

The Guardian Award provides special recognition each year for teams in Operations that best exemplify a Guardian spirit by supporting the safety and health of our Factory Family Members.

The Excellence in Ministry Award recognizes the generous and committed efforts of Factory Family Members who use their time to improve the lives of others here at work, in their communities, and in the world.

Other awards are given periodically for exceptional performance, attendance, and term of service. We are very intentional in seeking ways we can honor people for their creativity and achievements. Certainly, if one of our employees receives an award related to our industry as a whole, or an award given by a vendor or customer, we find ways to trumpet that good news throughout the company!

STRONG EVIDENCE OF FAMILY

On September 12, 2001, we had amazing evidence of a "family" at work. On that day, across America, people had a craving to be with their families.

The day before, of course, terrorists had attacked Northeast America, wiping out two skyscrapers and seriously damaging the Pentagon. One attack was thwarted and that plane fell from the sky in our home state, Pennsylvania. These attacks disturbed millions upon millions of people across our nation with shock and fear. On September 12, tens of thousands of workers across America called in sick so they could stay at home and be close to their loved ones. Our nation was reeling from tragedy and filled with internal stress. We all felt a crying need to be with those who would care for us and with whom we could feel safe and loved.

While many companies across America had record-setting absentee rates on September 12, CARDONE Industries had one of the highest worker-attendance percentages in our company's history. One of our Factory Family Members told me, "This is where I feel safest. People here care about me, and I want to be with them now." Nothing could have made me feel prouder on that day.

QUESTIONS ONLY YOU CAN ANSWER

1. How would you or your employees describe the culture of your business?
2. Do you or your company have a process that identifies the frustrations or anxieties of your employees?
3. In what ways do you openly recognize and honor the achievements of your people?

7

Helping People Develop

Every Person Is a Diamond in the Rough

Those who are in business know Peter Drucker was to management what Walt Disney was to entertainment. Drucker wrote more than thirty books, taught thousands of students, and donated valuable consulting time to America's foremost industries before he died in 2005 at the age of ninety-five.

Drucker was a person I admired greatly, in part for his management concepts, but also because he was a great communicator who could reduce complex ideas into memorable one-liners. What many people do not know about Drucker is that he was also a man of strong biblical values. He believed in the Servant Leadership model of Jesus Christ. He had a fundamental belief in the worth and dignity of every person and continually reminded managers that employees are a resource, not a "cost." Drucker said this about the role of leadership (quoted in *The Daily Drucker*):

> Leadership is the lifting of a man's vision to higher sights, the raising of a man's performance to a higher standard, the building of a man's personality beyond its normal limitations. Figure out what each of your employees' or

colleagues' strengths are, and develop these strengths to help people perform better."[1]

I personally interpret this as the challenge of helping a person discover the reason God created him or her. A business role or a career can be a key aspect of a person's purpose and, therefore, a significant part of the person's spiritual journey.

> *"Help people reach their full potential. Catch them doing something right."*
> —KEN BLANCHARD AND SPENCER JOHNSON,
> *THE ONE MINUTE MANAGER*

Regardless of a person's position on an organizational chart, at CARDONE we believe *every* person is a leader, since all of us are observed by others and influence others by our actions. Every person can and should develop leadership skills. I certainly aspire to see that happen at CARDONE.

We have a long-standing saying at CARDONE: "People are diamonds in the rough." That is why one of our four corporate objectives is: *To help people develop.*

BASIC LIFE SKILLS

In the early days, my father would gather people at a work station to talk to them about the principles of our business, relating ways they could apply those principles to their work and lives. This basic training was foundational to our business and helped many people develop and grow within the business.

We offered optional classes in our factories, which were aimed at giving employees basic life skills, such as showing them how to take care of simple home maintenance projects. This was important to our workforce, because many of our workers had never owned a house before. We challenged our accounting firm to offer free classes on money management, and we also brought in teachers to show our employees how to prepare tax returns.

The legal immigrants in Philadelphia we hired in the early days did not always understand the English language, but they were eager to work, learn, and develop. Some were educated in their own nations with degrees or technical training. They often spoke English poorly, so we brought in teachers to help our people learn how to speak, read, and write in English. In fact, translation was one of the roles that our chaplaincy program filled in the early days. Many of the people who worked for CARDONE in those early years will tell you that they appreciated working for a company who cared about them and their development.

> *"The task of an executive is not to change human beings. Rather, as the Bible tells us in the parable of the talents, the task is to multiply the performance of the whole by putting to use whatever strength, whatever health, whatever aspiration there is in individuals."*
>
> —PETER DRUCKER, *THE EFFECTIVE EXECUTIVE*

DEVELOPMENT OF A PERSON'S FULL POTENTIAL

While I believe a person is ultimately responsible for his or her own development, businesses should provide their employees opportunities for development. I also believe when a company looks for what is right with people and focuses on their strengths, a person's full potential can be developed. When a company's objective is to help people develop, it's only natural to look to promote people within the organization instead of looking for talent outside the business. Our approach has been to give an opportunity for growth and advancement to one of our own whenever possible. This promotes varied careers and career changes for our employees within our business. This approach builds trust and loyalty within an organization. It also offers hope. Our desire is for our people to *want* a long, fulfilling and, perhaps, highly varied career at CARDONE. The single greatest element in employee retention is giving employees opportunities for personal growth in areas of their personal strengths and we have been doing that for decades. We have found it's the best way to help people develop and build a business.

> *"Why is it that I always get a whole person, when what I really want is a pair of hands?"*[2]
>
> —HENRY FORD

Tom Rath, in his bestseller *Strengths Finder 2.0,* found that employees who have the opportunity to focus on their strengths and are developed in those areas are six times more likely to be engaged in their jobs and three times more likely to have an excellent quality of life.

Identifying and developing one's strengths is a diamond mine with huge payback potential for organizations. When we hire people, we look for three things: character, commitment, and a teachable attitude. We consider it *our* job to help employees discover their strengths and latent talents and we encourage them to aim higher for themselves. This approach is also instilled in our leaders.

Every business is looking for good people. In our early days it was especially challenging to attract good people with high potential. Those people, who risked their careers by coming with a start-up business like ours, trusted us to offer them development opportunities and we grew together. Let me give you just three stories of lives that have been "developed" at CARDONE.

George was a service manager at an installation shop. He started as a mechanic and worked into a managerial position. I knew George from church and admired his character, attention to detail, and documentation. I offered him a job and he came to work with us. I don't even recall George's first job at CARDONE, but he didn't stay in that job long. He quickly earned a promotion, and then another, and another. He wanted to learn, and he was teachable.

Today, George is responsible for corporate compliance and security for our business globally. He has dealt with great wisdom, confidence, and humility with the mayor of Philadelphia, the governor of Pennsylvania, and the United States Secretary of Commerce. He is doing far more than he ever envisioned he might do in his lifetime.

Luis arrived in the United States in the early 1980s. Three days after his arrival, he had a job at CARDONE. He had worked in drafting and electronics in his home nation, but the only job we could offer him at the time was disassembling blower motors.

It didn't take long for Luis's leader to recognize his skill. His hard work and his creative ideas for improving our methods came to the attention of those high in the organization. He was a fast learner with high technical aptitude. One of his first promotions was to a testing position in our motors division. He used his electronics knowledge and a few spare parts from Radio Shack to develop an electronic tester, which dramatically improved our product testing. We soon had Luis designing and building test equipment for many product lines. He became one of our top test equipment engineers.

Daniel and his wife immigrated to the United States from India in the late 1970s. Though Daniel had been part of the military and was a retired veteran from the India Air Force, he came to work with us in an entry-level position.

We noticed Daniel's ambition, work ethic, and ability to lead and organize. Daniel had the attitude, "Whatever is given to me, I'll do it. Whatever job comes my way, I'll do it with a full heart." Every day he came to work with the intention to do a "perfect job."

> *"'For I know the thoughts that I think toward you,' says the* LORD, *'thoughts of peace and not of evil, to give you a future and a hope.'"*
>
> —JEREMIAH 29:11

Daniel's leader gave him a "rush" project and one month to finish it. He had the project finished in a week. From then on, his rise in the company and leadership was rapid. Eventually, he became a plant manager, leading hundreds of our Factory Family.

During the 1980s and 1990s CARDONE expanded rapidly and Daniel was given a variety of assignments. He always completed his assignments with precision, excellence, and discipline.

One of the best things about Daniel is his appreciation of our interest in him and the opportunities we have given to him. In turn, he has taken great interest in helping many of our people develop.

These are just three of countless stories I could share. When employees are given the challenge to develop their potential, they tend to do so!

How exciting it is to discover an employee who has ambition and a willingness to work hard. If that person has the right character, commitment, and a teachable attitude, that person has a bright future at CARDONE.

THE DYNAMICS OF CONTINUALLY OPENING UP ENTRY-LEVEL POSITIONS

As leaders, I wholeheartedly believe one of the greatest challenges we face is helping people develop and improve their skills so they can advance and be in position to earn more money and build a better life for themselves and their families. We do them a great disservice when we keep them locked in entry-level jobs.

We Seek to Help People Develop

Because we value our people we help them develop by:

- Encouraging a spirit of teamwork
- Challenging them to stretch their abilities
- Fostering an atmosphere of constant positive change
- Providing leadership and educational support for career advancement

Leaders who deny their people the opportunity to develop new skills or advance are holding people back from developing. Some poor leaders don't want to lose what they have invested in the person, or they do not want to train someone else. In either case, the end result is poor, self-serving leadership, which causes both the employee and our business to lose.

One way we can help employees in lower paying, entry-level positions is to offer them development opportunities so they can qualify for advancement, rather than recommending they take on a second or third job. This generally means encouraging and offering various ways for them to develop skills and take advantage of technical training. The vast majority of people in today's workforce are likely to be called upon to do something in the next five to ten years they aren't currently doing, or have never done before. They will need to *be flexible and adaptable to learn new and different jobs*. It's been said that today's top ten jobs will not be the same or in the same order in just a few years.

In the May 31, 2004, issue of *Business Week*, the cover story "Working . . . and Poor" dealt with a statistic reported by the Census Bureau that stated 63 percent of all U.S. families who were living below the federal poverty line had one or more employed *workers* in the family. This confirmed that our nation had more than twenty-eight million low-paid workers.

What can companies do to help change this? We can promote workers on the basis of their skill development and performance, rather than increasing their salaries on the basis of their longevity with the company! We've been doing this at CARDONE for more than three decades and this principle works.

When people are given an opportunity to develop, those with ambition and a strong work ethic nearly always jump at that opportunity. If people are highly motivated to learn more, they usually earn more.

People who are given an opportunity to learn and advance

have an intuitive sense they are more highly *valued* by their employers. In return, they tend to value others more highly and to develop deeper loyalty to their employers.

The net result is workers stay longer with a company that develops them and continuing development becomes a way of life for them. They provide living examples for those in entry-level positions, showing advancement is possible; so go for it and give it your all.

This creates an overall atmosphere of hope and progress. The results are beyond anything that can be stated on a profit-and-loss statement. Valuing people by helping them develop, while focusing on their strengths and what's right with a person, promotes a positive and productive environment where people and business grow.

What If . . . .

I have thought long and hard about how Jesus recruited his team of twelve disciples. He didn't go to the seminaries of his day or to the temple in Jerusalem. He didn't go to the synagogue scholars. Rather, he chose twelve men who included fishermen, tent makers, lawyers, doctors, family members, and people of little notoriety. Jesus trained them to be His followers, and the results transformed the world. He chose them for their character, commitment, and teachable attitude.

What might have happened had Jesus followed accepted business practices in His recruitment? He might have received a letter such as this one from a headhunting consultant:

Dear JC:

Thank you for submitting the resumes of the twelve men you have picked for managerial positions in your new organization. All of them have now taken our battery of tests, and we have not only run the results through our computers, but also arranged personal interviews for each of them with our psychologist and vocation aptitude consultant.

We regret to inform you, it is the opinion of the staff that most of your nominees are lacking in background, education, and vocational aptitude for the type of enterprise you are undertaking. They do not have the team concept. We would recommend that you continue your search for persons of experience in managerial ability and proven capacity.

We have summarized the findings of our study below:

- Simon Peter is emotional, unstable, and given to fits of temper.
- Andrew has absolutely no quality of leadership.
- The two Zebedee brothers, James and John, place personal interests above company loyalty.
- Thomas demonstrates an inquisitive attitude that would tend to undermine morale.
- Matthew has been blacklisted by the Greater Jerusalem Better Business Bureau.
- James, son of Alphaeus, and Thaddeus definitely have radical leanings. Additionally, they both registered high scores on the manic depressive scale.
- However, the scores of one of the candidates indicates

great potential. He is a man of ability and resourcefulness. He is a great networker, has a business mind, and has strong contacts in influential circles. He is highly motivated, very ambitious, and adept with financial matters. We recommend Judas Iscariot as your Controller and Chief Operating Officer.

All other profiles are self-explanatory. We wish you the utmost success in your new venture.

Sincerely,
Jordan Management Consultants[3]

QUESTIONS ONLY YOU CAN ANSWER

1. How does your company help people grow and develop their full potential?
2. Does your company focus on and value your strengths?
3. In what ways do you actively seek to develop people so they might be prepared for leadership?
4. Does your organization offer educational or professional development opportunities?

8

Three Traits for the Job

Who You Hire Becomes Your Reputation

In the very early days of our company, my father hired Tony, a barber, because Dad thought Tony would be an excellent buyer of used car parts we call cores. Core buyers go out through the country dealing with salvage yards and core brokers. There are no published price sheets and the buying is a wheel-and-deal activity. It can be a down-and-dirty business, literally and physically. Tony was a meticulous dresser who always had manicured nails and liked things to be in good order. He was squeaky honest and could really split pennies. Tony was about the last person I would ever have imagined as a core buyer!

My father hired Tony not for his outward appearance, but for his character. Tony turned out to be one of the best core buyers in the business. Not only did he have a shrewd eye for getting cores at great prices, but he also kept a close eye on our inventories. If he felt we were overstocked in an item, he'd let us know. If he thought the quality of cores wasn't good enough—perhaps the items had been batted around too much—he'd pass up a deal, even if the price was low.

Since core buying is a matter of negotiation, it is very easy for core buyers to become dishonest, agreeing to one price with the person selling the cores, quoting a higher price to the person buying the cores, and pocketing the difference. We could always trust Tony to be impeccably honest.

As I watched Tony through the years, I became convinced that having the right college education or background experience wasn't what made a person "suitable" for a particular job. Character, commitment, and having a teachable attitude, a willingness to learn, and the ability to adapt to a new skill were the most important traits a person could possess.

Although we may not have been able to state it in the clear terms we use today, at CARDONE we have always had this approach to hiring:

Hire for character, commitment, and a teachable spirit.

If people have these three traits, they have what it takes to be able to learn how to do anything they want to do and we need them to do. I also believe that God has a person to help us with every problem we face. If we ask God for direction, and then look and listen to Him, we will find the person He has for us.

WHO WE HIRE, AND WHY

Any company can hire "talent" by working with headhunters, consultants, or through want ads. We hire:

- Character: honesty, integrity, work ethic, and values
- Commitment: determination, persistence, relationship building, and a commitment to our business culture

- Teachable spirit: willingness to learn and adapt to changes and a desire to develop

This does not mean we bypass educational and professional achievement when we hire new employees. Rather, it means we look for *more* than educational degrees and professional experience on a printed resume. When we review resumes, we don't just look to see who people are, but we try to envision what they can become.

A person can acquire skills and information *on the job*. Character, commitment, and a teachable attitude are inner traits a person must bring *to the job*. These traits cannot be taught, but they can be "caught." People in your company who model these traits influence others in the organization. Having the right kinds of role models in a business encourages those around them to develop and express the positive qualities they may already possess inside themselves.

> *"We have more people who want to do the right thing than most companies. We don't just look at experience. We want to know: Who are they? Why are they? We find out who they are by asking them why they made decisions in their life. The answers to these questions give us insight into their core values."*[1]
>
> —DAVID NASSEF, PITNEY BOWES

In the hiring process employers should look for people who already buy into the core values of the company. That is one of the reasons we are up-front in saying who we are and what we believe. This gives prospective employees an opportunity to see if they want to be part of our culture. If you take a look at our

Web site, you will find we are very open about our objectives as a company.

While skills are learned and can be classified as "head" knowledge, I believe people's values come from their heart. When personal values are in sync with corporate values, there is a synergy created that further motivates people and advances the business.

At CARDONE we ask Factory Family Members to help us recruit people who share our values and work ethic. We ask them to look for people they think would appreciate our work environment and enjoy being a part of our Factory Family.

Since we hire people to be a part of our family, we look for people who are committed to their own families. We have found people with a strong commitment to family are motivated not only for personal reward, but also for the benefit of their families and friends at work.

Through the years we have also found those who are attracted to our corporate values enjoy their working relationship with us. This works out best for them and us, because when there is unity in values, there is greater synergy in the workplace. We have also observed values-driven people are open to serving others. They build up the workplace, work well with others, and further strengthen our business culture.

A TEST OF OUR POLICY

Our approach to hiring was given a serious test in the 1990s. Until that time, we did not have our own sales force. Instead, we relied on a group of manufacturers' agents to represent us to our customers across the United States and Canada. As an outsourced sales force, these agents functioned as independent businesses and worked strictly on commission. They not only represented us, but they represented multiple small companies.

For almost twenty-five years these agents did a fine job of representing our products. They did not, however, understand, embrace, or reflect our values in their business practices and relationships. In all fairness, the fact that they represented many different companies at the same time made it almost impossible for them to do so. For the most part, they were outstanding salespeople who had only one focus: commission.

These agents were our primary point of contact with our customers, and for many of our customers, these agents were *all* they knew about CARDONE. As time passed, it became increasingly important for us to work with people who would reflect our corporate culture to our customers.

> *"Organizations whose success hinges on high-quality human interaction generally pay close attention to soft qualities when recruiting, hiring, and managing staff—empathy, flexible thinking, and a 'strong inner core'—qualifications that a resume does not reveal."*
>
> —David Bornstein, *How to Change the World: Social Entrepreneurs and the Power of New Ideas*

Several trends converged in the 1990s. Over the years, we had continued to expand our product lines to include more complex technical products, such as automotive electronics. Not all of the agents were as knowledgeable as we needed them to be in this area. In addition, we were fast becoming a major supplier in the market. Our business had grown to the point where we *could* support our own dedicated and trained sales force. Our salespeople would sell only CARDONE products and would reflect our corporate values.

Developing our own sales force was a challenging decision. Implementing this required countless hours, a huge expenditure of energy, and a significant amount of money. And there was significant risk in doing this.

From the start we applied our three-part criteria. When hiring the sales force, we looked for character, commitment, and a teachable spirit. We looked for people who shared our values. We knew if they shared our values and had these three traits, we could teach them what they needed to know about our products and processes.

Although it may have seemed like common sense to seek out salespeople within our own industry, we purposefully chose *not* to hire people from our competition, solicit at trade shows, or advertise in trade publications. For our sales force, we looked for people who were interested in a work environment that was congruent with their own personal values. We hired some people from outside our industry. These individuals shared our values and brought a fresh perspective to our business. Since some of them came from companies that did not have a values-based culture, they appreciated our emphasis on values, brought a renewed awareness of the importance of our values, and gave a tremendous boost to our belief that values are directly related to the achievement of excellence. Their enthusiasm has added to the morale within our company, even as their creative ideas have promoted innovation and new ways of selling.

We asked for referrals from people we knew shared our values. I once heard it said, "Tell me who your friends are and I will tell you who you are." Candidates emerged from all over the country. Among the people we hired were a former candy salesman, a coffee salesman, and one who had been a copier repairman.

After we had hired our new team, we put each person through an intensive training course focused on our values, our products, and our industry. Then, we turned them loose. As we sent out our salespeople, I told them, "If you don't know what to do, begin to wipe the customer's shelves, sweep the floor, or line up our product boxes in neat order. Do something that meets a customer's need and helps build a relationship based upon service and trust." We charged them to follow the Servant Leadership model of Jesus and be servants to our customers. We were confident that if they did this, the rest of what they needed to know and do would come in time.

PEOPLE ARE PARAMOUNT

Business practices are dead without people committed to carrying them out. We believe that in order to keep our business strong and unified we must:

- Create jobs that make the most of individual talents.
- Hire "family members"—people whom we can call family and who desire to be called family.
- Respect the diversity of our employees.
- Seek to develop employees to their highest potential.
- Respond urgently to employee needs.
- Reward performance.

They did what we trained and challenged them to do, and it worked! Initially, there was some resistance. One customer called and chided me for replacing the seasoned sales agents with inexperienced people. Over time, however, our new salespeople proved themselves to our customers. They showed up early for appointments. They were humble-spirited, listened to and served our customers, and eventually they built strong and trusting relationships with them. Frankly, I don't believe this approach had ever been used before in our industry.

On his first day making sales calls, one of our new salesmen, Vern, called on the customer who had chided me for hiring inexperienced people. Vern introduced himself and admitted he was new, but he also said, "I'm a fast learner." He then went right to the warehouse and began dusting shelves, because that was all he *knew* to do.

It wasn't long before this customer began to take notice of Vern's unusual but consistent behavior. He was doing things that no other salesperson had ever done, including the seasoned sales representatives!

A year later I received a phone call from this customer. He apologized to me for characterizing Vern as an inexperienced, immature salesperson. He went on to admit he had learned a big lesson he would never forget. He said he would never hire from within the industry again. He had seen a person, like Vern, who had character, commitment, and was teachable, deliver incredible results the best he had ever seen in a salesman. Today, our sales force is recognized throughout our industry as one of the best. They are noted for their commitment to values and dedication to service.

HAVING THE RIGHT PEOPLE ON BOARD

The statistics related to our hiring policies are verified in a number of ways.

- CARDONE does *not* spend a lot of money recruiting new workers. In fact, our best recruitment tool is our own people. They let us know when they think they have found somebody appropriate for our company.
- CARDONE has high employee loyalty, which means we have low rates of employee turnover. This translates into less time and expense in hiring and training new employees. Turnover is very costly.
- CARDONE has low absenteeism and tardiness rates, which results in increased productivity and, in turn, translates into lower cost per unit.
- CARDONE has a lower rate of injuries, a lower number of people in the Workmen's Compensation System, and we have long been recognized in the state of Pennsylvania for offering our workers one of the finest return-to-work programs.

Finding the combination of character, commitment, and a teachable spirit in people who have shared values and are focused on common corporate goals produces incredible results. If you get it right with the people inside the business, you will get it right outside in the marketplace.

QUESTIONS ONLY YOU CAN ANSWER

1. What do visitors see when they visit your place of business? What impressions will they take away after seeing your people at work?
2. When you hire, how heavily do you weigh the factors of character, commitment, and teachable spirit?
3. How can you get more of the right people on board with you?

9

The Search for Significance

The Key Lies in What Your Employees Call Significance

I recently received the following e-mail from one of our Factory Family Members working in Procurement.

> Michael:
>
> Prior to my career at CARDONE, I worked for a number of years for a man who served the priorities of this world—money, prestige, and self-importance. Through this time I had a longing to work for a values-based company. I didn't even know if any existed. I found CARDONE and have now worked here for more than a decade. Your philosophy of business has given me the significance I was looking for. Thank you.

Our shop steward, Fatima, recently retired after thirty-three years of working with us. She wrote me this meaningful letter:

> I came to America with my family, five pieces of luggage, and a lot of dreams. You made many of those dreams a reality. I accomplished many goals serving others. The opportunities you gave me were extraordinary and they made me a better

person. Even though I will retire, my heart is still with our company, and I will always be just a call away.

I can't begin to tell you how much I value messages such as these. Knowing our company makes a positive impact on another person's life and family has added significance to my life.

Numerous studies have shown that people today are looking to their employers for more than a paycheck. They are looking for purpose and meaning in their work. The challenge facing those in leadership is determining what *employees* regard as significance.

WHAT DO EMPLOYEES CALL SIGNIFICANT?

Virtually all employees want to do work that is "meaningful" to them. They want to contribute to something valuable, good, and necessary. They want to know they are making a difference in the company, with the customer, and in the community.

The Herman Trend Alert article titled "Social Responsibility Is Good Strategy" (May 7, 2008, from the Herman Group) concluded: "When employers give their people opportunities to make a difference . . . workers feel more 'bonded' to the organization." The report cited companies such as Coca-Cola, which works with Greenpeace to eliminate carbon emission from its vending machines and coolers. The overall trend is one in which employees have a growing desire to work for companies that are "good corporate citizens."

Some employees do not intuitively or automatically see the big-picture or significance of their work. As leaders it is up to us to help people make that connection so they can see *how* their work impacts others and their world. When they make this connection, they appreciate their work and draw meaning from what they do.

> *"What man actually needs is not a tensionless state but rather, the striving and struggling for some goal worthy of him."*
> —Viktor E. Frankl, *Man's Search for Meaning*

Here are some meaningful contributions our employees are making through their work. As remanufacturers of automotive parts, CARDONE is helping people across America and elsewhere maintain the cars they drive to and from work every day. We are helping people who drive trucks to deliver medical supplies for disaster relief, goods and services directly related to food distribution, building supplies, and manufacturing. We are helping to keep the world moving.

In addition, we are helping people reduce the cost of repairs to their vehicles. Remanufactured auto parts are one of the few recycled products that actually cost less to the consumer than a new part. That is quite an accomplishment, especially when one considers the additional costs associated with achieving greater environmental benefits.

The Automotive Aftermarket Industry Association reports that the average age of the passenger car and light truck on the road today in the U.S. is 9.7 years old.[1] People are holding on to their cars longer. The vehicles serviced by a CARDONE part are usually five years and older. The owners of these older vehicles need a lower cost alternative than the more expensive new part. A remanufactured part gives the owner the opportunity to keep the cost of repairs lower. Because our remanufacturing process corrects inherent weaknesses in a part, we offer a lifetime warranty. Plus, in the remanufacturing process we are creating jobs—more jobs than manufacturing a new part. When you also consider we put 10 percent of our profits back into the communities where we have our operations, it all adds up to *significance*!

On top of all this, CARDONE has a distinct "green significance" when it comes to environmental and economic concerns that impact our planet. Our remanufacturing process greatly reduces our carbon footprint.

When the United States entered World War II, daily life changed in countless ways for Americans. Every homemaker was aware of the implications that rationing had on her daily menus—items such as eggs, milk, and beef products were severely limited. Any person who owned a car knew about shortages of gas and rubber for tires, and the need for fuel conservation. Out of necessity, industrial products were also rationed. In fact, World War II marks the beginning of the era of remanufacturing, as our nation directed its natural resources to the war effort.

Long before there was a modern-day environmental movement or concern about greenhouse gases, remanufacturers, like CARDONE, were busy working to save the planet. Consider these facts published by Rolf Steinhilper in "Remanufacturing: The Ultimate Form of Recycling":

- Remanufacturing conserves 85 percent of the material and energy that would have been used to create the same volume of new products.
- Remanufacturing saves four hundred trillion BTUs of energy a year in our nation.
- Some seventy-three thousand remanufacturing companies exist in the United States with combined sales of more than $53 billion. As a whole, America's remanufacturing

> industry employs nearly a half million Americans, which is more than the steel industry.[2]

I'm proud of being a remanufacturer and I want all of our Factory Family Members to be proud of the contributions they are making too.

The Asia-Pacific Economic Cooperation of 2009 revealed companies from varied industries, like Caterpillar, Dell, Xerox, and GE, are taking a leading role in advancing global remanufacturing. These successful companies understand that reman not only makes good economic sense for the individual consumer, but remanufacturing may very well be a major economic wave in our world.

SIGNIFICANCE IN VALUES

All around us we see trends that mark changes in the business world. Instead of picking up a volume of an encyclopedia to find information, we do a Google search. Rather than going to a store to buy records for a record player, I download tunes to my computer or personal listening device. I also carry a phone that allows me to send and receive text messages.

Technology doesn't stop changing, but values are timeless. Lasting values are not linked to fads, styles, trends, or technological advances.

One day I accompanied our chaplains on a home visit to a woman whose husband had died. She and her husband had worked in our company for many years. During my visit in her home, she said, "Thank you, Mr. Cardone, for coming to pay your respects. But I want to thank you for more than that. You gave my husband and me our first job when we arrived in the United States, even though we did not speak English. Your company not only helped us improve the quality of life for our family, but we learned important values at CARDONE. The values we learned at work, we brought home and taught to our three daughters, including the values of quality, productivity, and integrity. My husband never lost a day of pay for twenty-three years and it was his steady job and the values we gave to our daughters, which made our daughters who they are today."

> *"I have concluded that the accumulation of wealth, even if I could achieve it, is an insufficient reason for living. When I reach the end of my days, a moment or two from now, I must look backward on something more meaningful than the pursuit of houses and land and machines and stocks and bonds. Nor is fame of any lasting benefit. I will consider my earthly existence to have been wasted unless I can recall a loving family, a consistent investment in the lives of people, and an earnest attempt to serve the God who made me. Nothing else makes much sense, and certainly nothing else is worthy of my agitation."*[3]
>
> —Dr. James Dobson, Founder of Focus on the Family

She then pointed to her mantel, where photographs of her daughters had been placed. She introduced me to her daughters one by one. As this proud mother spoke, I learned all three of their girls had gone to college and were outstanding young women.

THE LINK BETWEEN SIGNIFICANCE AND SELF-WORTH

There is a direct link, in my opinion, between significance and self-worth. When people are valued, they value themselves. When they are in an environment that promotes self-worth, they attach greater significance to that environment.

People who gain self-worth develop self-confidence. Very often, that translates into a desire to take on more responsibility, pursue personal growth, and develop themselves by learning new information and acquiring new skills to take on new challenges.

Years ago we had an employee who showed great promise. He was a hard worker and a quick learner, but he lacked confidence. As a result, he did not *want* to pursue leadership training. Eventually, he was offered and accepted a position as a department leader. The new job provided a desk. To our surprise, he kept his old work clothes under his desk, just in case he failed as a leader and had to return to his old job.

One day, his leader noticed the bundle of clothes under his desk and asked about them. When the employee explained why he kept them there, his leader said, "I understand your fear, but have confidence. I won't let you fail in this job!" When I heard that story, I was extremely proud of the leader, who showed his support and gave assurance to a rising, but fearful employee.

A PLACE YOU ARE PROUD TO CALL YOUR COMPANY

People also find significance in working for a company with a positive reputation. A company's reputation becomes part of an employee's personal reputation. Where a person works says something about the person. *The Economist* magazine recently reported the results of a survey that indicated more than 50 percent of employees consider a company's "good brand reputation" as an important "employee benefit."

A while back, I attended a Philadelphia City Council meeting to address a routine business issue. One of the newer councilmen began attacking CARDONE as a corporate tyrant. His accusations struck me as utterly bizarre and I didn't know how to respond. As it turned out, I didn't have to respond.

The secretary to the council is usually taking minutes and is stone silent at these meetings. This time was different. She had a number of relatives who worked for us, and she knew a great deal about us and how we operate. This brave woman stood up and took issue with the councilman who attacked us. She shared with the city council the positive influence we had on her family and on the community. She said what I would have liked to say, only far better.

Our company has been recognized by several of the communities in which we operate as someone who contributes to society and gives back. That honor gives added significance to all of us who work at CARDONE.

King Solomon has been called the wisest man who ever lived. He wrote, "A good name is more desirable than great riches." He was right!

QUESTIONS ONLY YOU CAN ANSWER

1. Do people in your workplace feel their work is significant?
2. What are some ways you can help workers view their jobs in a broader context so they see their work is meaningful?
3. What do people think or say about your company?

10

Making Factory Space a Special Place

Pleasant Space Produces Productive, Profitable Business

Our home city of Philadelphia has a lengthy history as a manufacturing city. I take great pride and satisfaction in knowing CARDONE Industries is currently the largest manufacturing company in Philadelphia. I am also keenly aware *most* people do not think of factories as being great working environments.

Making our plants a good place for our Factory Family to work is a top priority. It is a basic yet essential way we display value and respect to our employees. We know that it is the right thing to do, plus it inspires maximum productivity:

A high-quality environment is
directly related to high-quality performance.

HALLMARKS OF A HIGH-QUALITY ENVIRONMENT FOR HIGH-QUALITY WORK

We have more than 2.75 million square feet of plant space in our Philadelphia operations. It is a top priority that our work spaces have:

- *Good lighting*—This may seem rudimentary to some readers, but it's not. Insufficient light not only hinders worker productivity, but makes the workplace more dangerous. For this reason we provide almost double the amount of lighting required by industry standards. We know that light makes people feel better and more productive.
- *Fresh paint*—Walls and ceilings are kept freshly painted and clean.
- *Clean-air exchanges*—It is important that our workers breathe healthy, fresh, and clean air; so we have fresh air exchanges in all operations.

CLEAN AND ORDERLY

Over the years, as various companies have left Philadelphia for the suburbs, we have had a number of opportunities to buy their vacated facilities to meet our growing manufacturing needs. Before we occupy the space and begin operations in these buildings, we completely renovate them to meet *our* specifications. Part of our renovation is to make things clean and orderly. We beautify each facility inside and outside.

My father often repeated the old adage, "Cleanliness is next to godliness." Through the years I saw my father begin to address a problem in one of our production lines by *first* grabbing a broom and making the work area more tidy and orderly. He instilled in me a deep desire to see our factories kept neat and clean.

We stress cleanliness at all times. Employees are responsible for cleaning their work areas. Team leaders keep common areas in top-notch shape. Janitors are responsible for cleaning locker rooms and restrooms only. To ensure and inspire cleanliness in all areas, we have quantifiable housekeeping audits.

> *"We need to understand and be 'at home' in our working environment—both the human environment and the physical environment. There needs to be a visible order and a 'sense of place,' so that we may know who we are and where we fit. Our environments should have a human scale, and we have a right to beauty."*
>
> —MAX DEPREE, *LEADERSHIP IS AN ART*

Over the years we have adopted several unique sayings to support our cleanliness and orderliness standards:

- "A place for everything and everything in its place"
- "Nothing in the aisles and nothing on the floor"
- "Everything neat and straight like soldiers in a row"

The last five minutes of every shift is spent on "broom time." This is a unique CARDONE policy. This means every worker cleans up for the next shift. Our employees take pride in maintaining their work areas. The floor of an area is often the best indicator in a factory as to whether the work area as a whole is clean. You will find clean floors at CARDONE!

OPERATIONAL EXCELLENCE!

Cleanliness and orderliness are part of Operational Excellence at CARDONE. Cleanliness provides the foundation for safety, quality, and productivity.

Like other companies, we undergo audits by the federal government's Occupational Safety and Health Administration (OSHA). The first comment made by auditors usually pertains to the cleanliness and orderliness of our plants. It is also the first thing customers and suppliers comment upon when they take tours. Cleanliness and orderliness are a reflection of our values. I believe people "hear with their eyes" before they ever hear with their ears. We actually welcome these audits as part of our continuous improvement process.

A SAFE ENVIRONMENT PHYSICALLY AND EMOTIONALLY

We do everything we can to promote workplace safety. OSHA regulates safety in the workplace but at CARDONE, we have adopted a Zero Injury Policy, which goes far beyond OSHA's mandates. We are passionate about worker safety. To that end we:

- Conduct regular training for supervisors and employees so every person knows our policies and procedures.
- Ask all of our employees to be on alert at all times for ways in which we might improve a function or area for greater safety.

We have trained first aid responders in every work area. When there is an injury, we fully investigate the situation, conducting interviews with all those involved. Then, we implement the changes necessary to prevent injuries and develop a fully safe work environment. Safety involves more than cleanliness, fire extinguishers, and evacuation routes. An environment isn't truly safe to a person unless that environment "feels" safe. Everything related to safety is proactive, intentional, trained, and clearly understood by all Factory Family Members.

One of our foremost solutions for clear understanding has been our continued effort to document every process in our factory and to communicate these through pictures or illustrations. This is part of our methodology for addressing safety and health concerns as well.

Going the extra mile in the area of safety is a small investment compared to a potentially huge payoff. We have significantly lower rates of worker injuries than other companies in our industry and we believe it is directly related to the value we place on people and safety.

ESTABLISHING SOCIAL AND SPIRITUAL SPACE

At each of our CARDONE factories, we have designated social and eating areas. We encourage people to eat on the premises, in designated areas, for these reasons: to provide healthy food choices, to decrease tardiness after lunch and other breaks, and to give people greater opportunity to mingle together and forge friendships. This, in turn, produces higher morale and greater loyalty within our business.

We also have designated meeting areas that we call chapels. These areas are used for departmental meetings, staff training, and other meetings. Our chapels are also used for periodic, off-the-clock times for prayer and meditation.

We believe these spaces are vital to helping workers connect with one another and share aspects of their lives that lie primarily beyond the workplace. Some of our employees have held their weddings in our chapels. Others have used these spaces for funerals of family members. Dedicating and using space for these purposes may seem to be unprofitable in sheer income-generating terms. Overall, however, it is one of the best things we do to help promote and facilitate a family culture.

We do not substitute social time for work time. We are very serious about each employee giving an honest day's work for an honest day's wage. We all understand that, unless we stay focused and highly productive in our work, we won't have a workplace! At the same time, in creating opportunities for employees to build relationships with one another, our employees are also creating a stronger relationship with the company as a whole. They see CARDONE as more than an employer. It is a *place* where they are safe emotionally and physically. For some, the workplace is a safer place than their homes, apartment buildings, or neighborhoods.

EXCELLENCE IN ENVIRONMENT

We support a work environment marked by the following elements:

- Every person has value and worth and should be treated with dignity and respect.
- Every person should have a safe and healthy work space.
- Leaders are to be in touch with their workers.
- Providing a wholesome atmosphere is important.
- Celebration and a sense of humor are encouraged.
- Our employees are entitled to union representation and

our management is strongly committed to working with union leaders.

We ask and encourage the following traits in our employees:

- Flexibility
- Teamwork
- Accountability
- Sense of ownership

THE POWER OF POSITIVE SPACE

A positive physical space readily translates into a mind-set of excellence. That atmosphere must be reinforced with positive leadership. Together, the tangible positive work space and the intangibles of positive behavior create an overall workplace that is "positive." When a workplace is perceived as positive, you'll notice two great benefits:

1. People Report Experiencing Less Stress

Those who feel less stress on the job produce higher quality products, give better customer service, have lower absentee rates, have fewer accidents, and report higher morale. These factors, in turn, produce lower workmen's compensation costs, lower health-care costs, lower employee turnover rates, and reduced recruitment and training costs.

An article entitled "Absenteeism and the Bottom Line" reports that companies with low morale need to designate 5.3 percent of their budgets to dealing with stress-related consequences, while companies with good morale only need to designate 3.7 percent.[1] Good morale is cost effective!

One particular study of "unhealthy" workplaces found that workers experience higher levels of stress and burnout when they work in an environment marked by interpersonal conflict, work/life imbalance, and unsupportive supervisors. Researcher Graham Lowe said such a workplace environment could account for as much as 20 percent of worker health-care costs.[2]

2. People Are More Productive

An article titled "A Little Attitude Adjustment Raises the Bottom Line" appeared in the March 2004 issue of the *Washington Business Journal*. It noted:

> Workplace conflicts cost US businesses an average of 25–30 percent of productivity per person, or 200 million workdays annually, and that doesn't include alcohol and drug abuse and overt violence. It also costs 65 percent of performance problems, which costs between $3–5 billion annually. That means 32 percent of a workweek is spent resolving conflict. Intimidated employees spend 10 percent to 52 percent of their time defending themselves or networking for support. Twenty percent of people problems waste at least 30 percent productivity of six other people's time and energy.

The creation of a positive physical environment has tremendous financial ramifications!

A SIMPLE TEST

If you're a leader in your company, I encourage you to do the job in your company you consider "least desirable," probably an entry-level job of some type.

Stay there for an hour. Ask yourself, "Would *I* like to spend my time in this work space?" If the answer is anything other than a resounding "yes," choose to make some changes to improve it. The truth is, if you don't like what you experience there in an hour, the workers who occupy that space eight hours a day, five days a week, probably don't like it either.

QUESTIONS ONLY YOU CAN ANSWER

1. Do your employees feel their workplace is a "positive" place?
2. Does your company meet or exceed acceptable standards for safety, cleanliness, and health?

11

Urgency Plus Persistence

Creating the Intangible Atmosphere for High Productivity

In the first months of CARDONE, we were humming along fairly well. Growth was slow but steady. We offered one product line: windshield wiper motors. We produced a good product at a fair price. We had a highly cohesive staff, consisting of my father, mother, wife, a handful of employees, and me!

Then, tragedy struck. During one of the coldest weeks in Philadelphia's history, we had a devastating fire. Ice from the firehose water covered the blackened ruins. The scene was one of utter desolation. We lost everything.

Since my father was on vacation at the time, I felt especially bad the fire and devastation had occurred "on my watch." When I reached Dad by phone, his first concern was for the personal well-being of all who worked at our start-up business. After he was assured nobody was injured, he said, "That's why we have insurance."

On the surface, the situation left all of us wondering, at least for a few hours, if trying to restart the business was the right thing to do. My wife, Jacquie, and I were working long hours, arriving in the dark in the early morning and going home in the dark at night. Suddenly, in a matter of a few hours, everything we had worked to accomplish, including all of our equipment and inventory, was lost.

When people talk euphemistically about their dreams "going up in smoke," I don't have to do much imagining. I know precisely what that looks like *in reality*.

> *"As a leader, I don't expect my people to know all the answers, but I do expect them to be fully aware of the problems they face."*
> —MICHAEL CARDONE JR.

Then, we began to see our situation in the light of what *might be* instead of what *had been*. That's an important paradigm shift we all need to make, not only in our businesses, but also in our personal lives. Jacquie and I both value the day we made that shift, moving from "wondering" to acting quickly with faith and confidence. We knew we could and would rebuild. To this day, what we experienced next I consider a series of amazing miracles.

I spent hours upon hours searching through the charred remnants with fire inspectors and insurance adjustors. As an insurance adjuster would hold up a charred part, he'd ask, "How much is this part worth? What does it do? Where did you buy it? How many did you have on hand?" I was expected to have all the answers in immediate recall.

Fortunately, our bookkeeping was done at home, so that was safe. Amazingly, Jacquie and my mother were able to recall many office details. They reconstructed customer orders, and we immediately began to call our customers.

We moved quickly to secure new space. Since our business was expanding, we had already been scouting potential properties. When I called to see if one particular building was still available, it was! It was located only a short distance from our old location and was ready for occupancy. As soon as my parents returned to Philadelphia, my father, mother, Jacquie, and I went to look at it. The lease for the building said it would be delivered "broom clean," which means nothing would be inside the structure. When we opened the door and turned on the light switch, big ceiling lights flooded the interior, revealing a building that was anything but "broom clean." It was dusty and cluttered with large packing crates and drums. None of us said anything for a moment. Then Dad and I looked at each other and in near unison said, "Perfect!"

We purchased several long planks at the lumberyard and carted them to the new building. We arranged the packing crates and barrels in rows and laid the planks across the top of them, creating instant worktables for our assembly lines. Those crates and drums just happened to be waist high!

Within three days of the fire, we were back in operation. The new building turned out to be even better than we had thought. The facility had a room with thick concrete walls, ideal for our processing equipment.

In beginning again, we upgraded our equipment and office systems. We quickly arranged for the delivery of everything necessary to restart our remanufacturing work, which included shipments of new component parts and the basic raw materials of our business, the old car-part cores.

There are some valuable lessons I learned during this time. Customers I thought were solidly in our corner before the fire quickly turned to our competitors for supply. For this reason I never take customer loyalty for granted and strongly believe customer loyalty is something that must be pursued diligently and cultivated with great care. In addition I learned a tremendous amount about insurance, far beyond anything I had learned in college.

Something inside me was forged through that fire. I learned firsthand that setbacks in business set the stage for great comebacks. When people are determined to succeed and refuse to quit, they will succeed.

From that point on, I took nothing for granted. As a result of the fire, we at CARDONE became acutely aware we are only as good as our last shipment to a customer. Additionally, through that fire experience, I learned the practice of persistence, a relentless drive that will not quit, is rooted in a positive and determined *can-do* attitude. Today's marketplace is a battlefield and only those who truly practice urgency and persistence are going to survive.

THE PRINCIPLE OF URGENCY

At CARDONE, the Principle of Urgency, in practice, might be translated this way: A problem that arises *today* must be addressed and resolved *today*. Urgency means you take action now to resolve the problem. This brings swift resolution to issues, freeing you to make new progress.

The Principle of Urgency, of course, not only addresses remanufacturing concerns. It also addresses people concerns. We seek to address every need, answer every question, and make every attempt to resolve each issue, the day it arises.

The element of speed is essential to our business model. Our customers want their products fast. When a car is down, there is an immediate need for the repair part. The Principle of Urgency creates *intensity and passion in your work.*

The Principle of Urgency demands:

- Take action now
- No procrastination
- No delay

Not all problems can be fully resolved immediately, but we take the position that we can *begin* to solve the problem right now, when it arises. Then, we must *persistently* address the issue until it is resolved. The combination of urgency and persistence produces a strong formula for personal and business success:

The Principle of Urgency
\+ *The Practice of Persistence*
= Problem Solved in the Shortest Time

I don't think my father ever faced a problem he thought was unsolvable and I have adopted that same perspective. When someone brought a difficult problem to my dad, he would say, "They went to the moon!" This meant, compared to the complexity of going to the moon, our problem is not all that difficult. We can and will solve this problem. If the problem is possible, so is its solution!

THE DUAL KEYS FOR HIGH PRODUCTIVITY

These two keys of urgency and persistence also help a business maintain what some have called "start-up fever." One of my favorite business books in recent years has been *Think Big, Act Small* by Jason Jennings. The title says it all. One of the ways a company can maintain momentum is to maintain its "early-days" enthusiasm, continually pushing the envelope, continually striving for more, continually recharging its "values" batteries, and continually renewing its commitment to the causes it regards as most important.

> *"Celebrate for a nanosecond, then move on."*[1]
> —Michael Dell, Dell Computers

Taken together, the Principle of Urgency and the Practice of Persistence create an energized and productive atmosphere. When cohesive teams of people focus on a common goal, pursue it with urgency, and work with persistence great things can be accomplished.

QUESTIONS ONLY YOU CAN ANSWER

1. To what degree is your workplace permeated with an atmosphere of *must-do* persistence toward your business goals?
2. To what degree is your workplace atmosphere marked by a sense of urgency that problems must be resolved quickly?
3. Have you clearly defined the common goal for your team?
4. How do you model persistence and urgency in your leadership?

12

Establishing Two-Way Communication

Your Employees Can Be Your Most Valuable Consultants

When I was chairman of Motors Equipment Manufacturers Association (MEMA), I had the opportunity to have dinner with the president of Toyota of North America Manufacturing. Japanese automotive companies such as Toyota have gained an increasing market share of the U.S. automobile industry. I believe their commitment to developing a strong and positive corporate culture is a significant factor in their success. In the automotive world, "The Toyota Way" is the standard of excellence many companies aspire to achieve. Toyota's consistent quality, focus on their customers, and the way they engage their employees is the envy of every auto manufacturer.[1]

As Toyota's president and I discussed our corporate cultures, I expressed my desire to maintain our CARDONE Industries culture across all operations and with all our employees as we continue our growth as a global, family business. Since Toyota successfully developed their corporate culture globally, I asked what advice he might have for us. Frankly, I expected he would either give me Toyota's detailed process or recommend a consultant. Instead, he gave me these four rather basic points:

- Keep it simple.
- Engage your people in the process.
- Create an environment in which your people can talk.
- Teach your people problem-solving.

I appreciated what he said and nodded in agreement as I reflected on the principles we have implemented at CARDONE, which are quite similar to those embraced by Toyota. My mind went back to the significance of a decision we made years ago, where we applied and incorporated those four principles in our business.

FIVE MINUTES THAT START THE DAY RIGHT

That key decision came at the end of 1978. We were growing rapidly. We had eight plants in operation with four hundred employees. We were remanufacturing wiper motors, distributors, master cylinders, power-steering pumps, control valves, and steering gears. And we were preparing to launch additional product lines, including power-brake boosters, blower motors, and, then, rack-and-pinion steering units.

Over the Christmas holidays we discussed the internal communication challenge we faced. Our sales, products, plants, organization, and employee head count were all growing exponentially. There was a sense of urgency to develop methods that would enable us to remain in touch with our Factory Family—to hear them and their ideas and to be aware of their problems. We wanted to maintain our people-first, performance-based, customer-focused, family culture and needed a solution that would foster communication with all our people.

> *"Quality Control Circles represent something which is bigger, much more fundamental to management, than quality control as it is understood in most western companies. The Circles are, basically, an effective means by which the senior managements of a large sector of Japanese industry have succeeded in involving their employees in the aims and the purpose of their enterprises. This involvement, and the special factors that have made the Quality Control Circle movement possible, are underlying reasons for Japan's rapid rate of progress."*[2]
>
> —FROM JAPAN QUALITY CONTROL CIRCLES

Our solution was a two-step process. First, we determined to meet with our leaders before work at 6:55 A.M. Our objective for this meeting was to unify our leadership and prepare them to communicate a single-focused message to our Factory Family Members. Second, at 7:30 A.M., when the workday begins, each leader would meet for five minutes with groups of ten to fifteen Factory Family Members.

These meetings were intended to help connect our people and provide vital two-way communication. Our leaders would communicate a positive thought for the day, show concern for each person, and provide time for workers to share their issues, problems, or ideas. At the end of the meeting, each group would read an inspiring Bible verse designated for that day and the meeting would close in prayer. Although no one was required to stay for the prayer, all would be paid for the time they spent in these meetings. We considered this to be a valuable investment of time and money in our Factory Family.

On the first day back to work from the Christmas and New Year holidays, we announced our new plan and kicked it off. We held our breath not knowing how people would react to it. After the first week the answer was clear. Our leaders were enthusiastic and our Factory Family was engaged. In those first five minutes of the day we talked about business issues and began to hear ideas to improve our business, products, and services. We were amazed at the feedback. We learned who was working in a drafty area, who had a nonfunctioning workstation, who had an idea about a better way to inspect parts, who was absent because their home was broken into, and countless other things.

When we studied Japanese manufacturing systems a few years later, we found many similarities between their "quality circles" and our inspiration meetings at the start of each day. In one sense, our meetings functioned like a football huddle, which brings players together for teamwork. From another perspective our meetings promoted continuous improvement, which is a key element of Quality Circles.

Two-way communication came out of the five-minute meetings and this ignited a new sense of camaraderie, as well as an open, "team" feeling throughout the business. We were in touch with our people in a more personal way and helped many of our Factory Family Members in practical ways. We helped them resolve problems; and in the end, our workforce became increasingly loyal, committed, and engaged. Since their inception, the first-thing-in-the-morning inspiration times have continued to develop. Today, we call them "Take 5" sessions and they still set the tone for our workdays.

Over the years we have continued perfecting these first-five-minutes-of-the-workday meetings. Now, we regularly prepare a "Take 5 Sheet" for leaders. On this sheet we remind them of the principles of effective meetings, furnishing them ideas on how to give continuity and structure to the meetings and listing essential topics we want them to address in each week's meetings. The Take 5 meeting consists of three parts: Welcome, Work, and Wisdom.

TAKE 5 TOPICS

The following list provides topics and summaries from some of our daily Take 5 meetings in recent years

A Fresh Start. Employees should make a plan for improving their lives and their work practices during the year. The plan should be specific in its goals, accountable and subject to re-examination during the year.

You Bring Change. Changes in the company come through workers like you, so take the initiative and when appropriate take risks. Don't just plan, but take action.

Customers Are Important. Customers are the main reason we have our jobs, so meet their needs and be enthusiastic. Change the idea that customers are an interruption to our work.

Honoring God. Our first corporate objective is to honor God. This means doing the right things, being a good steward, and caring for people.

Ethics. We want to do the right things because our first corporate objective is "*To Honor God.*" This meeting also reminded workers about the company's Ethics Hotline. Employees can call anonymously if they feel they are witnessing or being asked to do something that violates our commitment to ethics and integrity.

Environmental Policy. We routinely remind workers that CARDONE has been certified by the International Standards Organization with the ISO 14001 certification, which recognizes leading global companies in managing the environment. They are asked to do their part by making sure we have zero discharge (spills) and familiarizing themselves with our environmental policies.

Thirty-Five Years of Pursuing Excellence. This explains our historic passion for excellence. The company started out with this goal and now each employee must continue to pursue excellence.

How Can You Continually Improve? Keep improving so you can make a difference in the company. Eliminate waste. And when problems arise use the CARDONE 5-Step Corrective Action Process for addressing them.

May 19th – 23rd

Operations Edition

Questions or comments about Take 5? Call extension 3861.

Leaders Model the Culture

Welcome
- Create a positive atmosphere
- Get to know your team
- Recognize FFMs

Work
- Resolve issues
- Look for & implement solutions

Wisdom
- Read disclaimer
- Read scripture verse
- Prayer

CARDONE Industries does not discriminate on the basis of race, color, religion, sex, national origin, ancestry, age, marital or veteran status, the presence of non-job related disability or any other protected characteristic for purposes of continued employment, employee benefits, or promotion.

Mon. 5/19

ANNOUNCEMENTS

Weekly PMs are due today.

Next Monday, May 26th, is a company holiday for Memorial Day. To be paid for this time you must:
Have been hired on or before April 26th
Work your schedule on Friday, May 23rd.
And work your schedule on Tuesday, May 27th.

Town Hall Meetings are this week. Frank Z. will be available to answer any questions about the business during your lunch or after work:

Rising Sun: Today in RSC Chapel from 12:00 – 12:30 and 12:30 – 1:00.
Cores: Today in the chapel from 2:30 – 3:00.
Plant 20: Tomorrow in the large conference room from 11:30 – 12:00 and 12:00 – 12:30.
CDC Offices: Wednesday in the Audion from 12:00 – 12:30 and 1:00 – 1:30.
Distribution: Thursday in the lunchroom from 12:00 – 12:30
Plant 21: Friday in the chapel from 12:00 – 12:30.

Recognize FFMs, as appropriate.

Work ***Review metrics, ask for ideas to improve or eliminate waste (muda).***

Move It Forward

Moving forward is easy. It just requires change. Walt Disney once said, "We keep moving forward, opening new doors and doing new things. Moving forward is essential for a business to survive."

Let me encourage you today to really look at what you do. How could the things you do be done differently? Change things and move forward.

Wisdom ***Leaders state: "Attendance is not required for this portion of the meeting."***

Blessed is the man who always fears the LORD, but he who hardens his heart falls into trouble.
Proverbs 28:14 (NIV)

Intense Product Development. We let our employees know about our various initiatives each year that are designed to keep us ahead of the competition. Then we remind them to cut waste, lower costs, be creative, and share ideas on reducing waste and saving money.

Be Safe. Falls cause the greatest number of disabling injuries in offices, so we should clear the floors of boxes/wires, close file cabinet drawers, etc.

Top and Bottom Line Growth. To increase our sales and our profits, we need to have what the customer needs when they need it—so think outside the box.

Order-Fill Excellence. Following on the previous point, we state our goal of ever-improving order fill and ask our employees how they can improve order fill.

Protecting Our Factory Family Members' Hearts with AEDs. We explained the installation and utilization of cardiac defibrillators (AEDs) in all plants. Every forty-seven minutes in the U.S. someone dies at work from a heart attack. The key to survival is early defibrillation within the first four minutes of a heart attack. AEDs are an essential part of our broader safety program.

Help People Develop. Helping people develop is one of our four corporate objectives. Take charge of your own development and strengthen those around you.

How Can You Work Better? Our Quality Policy says "we will continually improve products and processes as the path to excellence." You can do this by being organized and staying organized in your work area.

Staying Motivated. Motivation starts with your own attitude. Just do it; connect it with bigger goals; and take daily steps.

Your Part in Quality. Quality means meeting customer requirements. So get to the root causes of problems. Don't repeat mistakes.

Your Work Matters. This is an encouraging talk on employees doing excellent work. Conclude by asking questions on how we can improve services and cut costs.

Building Great Teams. A successful team is made up of individuals working together toward a common goal. State goals clearly and follow solid tips on team building.

Raising the Bar on Performance. This meeting focused on how Asian manufacturers have increased their market share in the U.S. automotive aftermarket. Citing examples of what various Asian-based companies have done, we encourage our people to pursue continuous improvement in order to effectively compete.

Being a Servant Leader. We provide frequent repetition of this key aspect of CARDONE corporate culture. A main point is that a servant leader influences others not by title or power, but by who you are and the care you show for others.

Increasing Your Potential. People only use 10 percent of their potential, so increase to your true potential. Have a good attitude; look for opportunities; attempt the "impossible."

E-mail Communication Tips. Keep them short and edit them so they are clear. Remember that they're not a substitute for human communication. Always include your contact information.

Business Update. At various times during the year, we inform all our workers on aspects of new business plans or product lines that will keep them up to speed on what is happening in other areas.

Adding Value. These are ways to add value and meaning to your work.

Feedback Is the Breakfast of Champions. Continually learn by getting feedback. Good practices include listening, speaking up, and seeking feedback on your work.

Keeping Customers Satisfied. It costs five times more to get a new customer than to keep an old one, so let's focus on keeping current customers satisfied.

Living Healthier. Tips on how employees can have healthier lives through diet, exercise, not smoking, etc.

Managing Your Health Care. How employees can better manage their health care by having annual checkups; using preventative screenings, and taking generic drugs.

BIG IMPACT FROM A LITTLE MEETING

I regard the "Take 5" meetings we do each day as *official* opportunities to encourage communication, reinforce our corporate culture and values, express the value of meeting and exceeding our customers' requirements, and receive essential feedback from our Factory Family. Their feedback is essential, because they know best what is needed to improve their job and our business performance.

Ultimately, the meetings are about "giving and taking"; and we believe open channels for two-way communication are vital. At times, the leader is the primary giver of information, encouragement, and motivation. At other times, workers give and receive from one another. Then, there are times when the workers are the primary source of new ideas, where the team's performance becomes the focus. Such times create relationship and unity. There is not a precise formula or price tag for unity, but it is worth pursuing. Unity in the workplace is a valuable, significant asset to any business.

As I outlined earlier, at the end of each Take 5 meeting, we close with "wisdom," which is a voluntary time when we share a Bible verse and prayer. One person in the group volunteers to pray for the needs expressed by the group. We have found our employees appreciate this sincere care for each other. Though people are free to leave the meetings before the prayer time, few, if any, do so.

Some of our morning meetings move so fast that if you aren't quite awake or if you blink, you might wonder if you missed the meeting. On the majority of the mornings, however, Take 5 meetings are a warm, culturally coherent, and organized way to begin the first five minutes of the CARDONE workday.

DEVELOPING LEADERSHIP POTENTIAL

Some of our people had never led a meeting in their lives before they came to CARDONE and were given responsibility for a daily Take 5 meeting. We train our Take 5 leaders for this brief but important daily session. We want every Take 5 leader to:

- Be skilled at preparing and presenting a simple message
- Be able to run a meeting effectively and productively
- Communicate so that listeners truly *understand* a message, honoring differences and diversity in their communication

As part of their training, Take 5 leaders are trained and encouraged to JUMPSTART their meetings. This is a simple acronym for:

J = Jumpstart by being positive and focused.
U = Understand announcements and the key message.
M = Motivate others by being enthusiastic.
P = Practice: review the material beforehand.
S = Smile to create a comfortable atmosphere.
T = Translate and restate as necessary, but keep the message short and simple.
A = Ask for prayer requests and close in prayer.
R = Recognize people.
T = Time is important. Arrive early and finish on time.

OTHER COMMUNICATION VENUES

In addition to the communication occurring during Take 5s, we take full advantage of technology. We use a phone network for company-wide voice mail messages and make extensive use of e-mail via the company intranet. We also utilize several other methods of communication.

MONDAY MORNING MICHAEL

Each week I send out a Monday-morning broadcast to more than a thousand of our people who have voice mail. I follow up the voice mail message by sending the same message in e-mail format. This sets the tone for our weekly Take 5 themes.

W.O.W. MEETINGS

We have regularly scheduled W.O.W. (Workers of Worth) meetings, which focus on the state of our business and overall plant or a specific department's performance. These thirty-minute meetings are held regularly throughout the year. At these plant and divisional meetings we educate, give recognition, review performance metrics, and empower and encourage our employees. A variety of company reports are presented, including updates on quarterly performance indicators. Usually, I give a brief message by videotape, highlighting our Factory Family in action and addressing industry and business issues.

One-on-One Meetings

At CARDONE we have adopted a process for conducting one-on-one interviews that is based on Ken Blanchard's Situational Leadership II®. What is unique about these meetings is that the employee (not the leader) sets the agenda and desired outcomes, and the leader's role is to listen and provide information, direction, and support.

These meetings are a proven method for creating perspective, trust, relationship, and increased effectiveness. They are a means of maintaining corporate focus, goal setting, achieving corporate results, developing both individual employees and sharing responsibility within the corporation. They are also a means of modeling Servant Leadership, creating a culture of accountability for the leader and team member, as both pursue excellence within the organization.

One-on-One meetings are scheduled by the employee and provide opportunity for face-to-face communication between the Factory Family Member and his or her leader. The meetings are held at least once a month and provide a forum for feedback, problem-solving suggestions, direction, coaching, performance management, and personnel development. At CARDONE

Industries, all reviewable employees are required to have regularly scheduled One-on-One meetings with their leader. Records of these meetings are kept so that progress can be assessed from year to year.

The Factory Family Member sets the agenda for the One-on-One. A form is provided to create the agenda and both the leader and the team member have prescribed roles. It's the Factory Family Member's role to prepare the agenda for the meeting, using a form that is provided. This form is submitted to the leader prior to the meeting. The agenda identifies specific issues for which the Factory Family Member needs direction, coaching, support, and discussion on the topics he or she has chosen. The agenda should also include areas for future learning and growth. The goal of the agenda is to produce a plan of action with "next steps" identified for both the leader and the Factory Family Member.

The leader is asked to see the Factory Family Member as a whole person and should express this to the Factory Family Member by asking about the employee's family, recognizing the person's accomplishments, and praising their good work.

The Factory Family Member raises issues while the leader listens and gives direction, coaching, and or support based upon the Factory Family Member's development level. The leader may also provide direction to the Factory Family Member in determining metrics, projects, and providing information as to how each project links directly to corporate objectives.

Finally, the leader identifies areas for future growth and charts a plan of action with the Factory Family Member, reviewing the person's performance plan, learning objectives, and performance goals for the future. The leader's goal is to use the agenda items to develop the person, making him more productive as he gains experience in his work.

> *"I will bless the LORD who has given me counsel;*
> *my heart also instructs me in the night seasons."*
> —PSALM 16:7

BEYOND THE OPEN DOOR

Even though every person in leadership is expected to have an open door, including an open mind and heart, One-on-One meetings are a specific, intentional means of focusing on the individual needs of every person, which involves helping persons develop and achieve their personal, work, and corporate goals.

At CARDONE we take corporate communication seriously. We audit our Factory Family Members quarterly to measure our effectiveness in communicating corporate values and other vital business information. We do that by preparing four messages in a question-and-answer format for our leaders to communicate to their people. We also use our W.O.W. meetings and Take 5s to help reinforce the four messages. In essence, we are giving everyone the answers to the questions. Then, we randomly ask a sample of employees to answer the four questions. This gives us a score that shows us areas in which we are successful or need improvement. Then, we share the results with our leaders to show them the messages they need to re-communicate and we also suggest ways leaders can improve their communication.

QUESTIONS ONLY YOU CAN ANSWER

1. In what ways do you engage in *two*-way communication in your company?
2. How often do your employees hear from you?
3. How open is your door?

13

A Factory with Chaplains

An Organized and Accountable Expression of Honoring God and Valuing People

In the early days of our business, with a few dozen employees, we were able to personally know all of our people. We knew all their names, families, and problems. That's how we wanted it. We got involved because we cared about our people. This sincere care for our people resulted in high levels of motivation, loyalty, and excellence in work performance. That energy of unity fueled our growth as we worked together for our customers.

As we grew beyond the point where we knew each employee personally, we sought new ways to develop a close family environment in which trust and teamwork might continue at a high level. The Take 5 meetings were a key in creating an environment in which employees could share ideas and personal needs. We faced the challenge of how best to *address* the Factory Family's needs, which were shared throughout the day, while maintaining the work intensity needed in our business.

Our leaders began to say things like, "It's great to have people asking for prayer and advice on personal concerns, but I don't feel I'm all that qualified to answer." Another said, "People are asking me for counsel to the point I'm having trouble finding time to deal with work issues."

> *"To maximize the effectiveness and impact that our chaplains have with our Factory Family . . . we continually evaluate, assess, and adapt our methods and programs, but our principles and values surrounding our people remain constant."*
> —THERLOWE PAULIN, CARDONE DIRECTOR OF CHAPLAINCY

We saw clearly that we had to find a way of dealing with the dynamics of our competitive business environment and the compassion we felt for our people. We decided we needed a full-time person on our staff, someone who would be an extension of our heartfelt concern, yet trained to handle the personal problems our employees expressed, including their spiritual concerns. One of our leaders knew a wise, caring pastor, who was retiring from his church position. Within two weeks after we first expressed our need, Chaplain Pagano came on board to serve as our first chaplain.

We wanted Chaplain Pagano to be out with the five hundred or so people we employed at the time, so he circulated throughout the day, listening and keeping his eyes open for needs. He quickly became a trusted, safe confidant to our people and a valuable asset to our business. Even though he had no handbook and no job description, he had a heart for people and our support to meet the challenges of being there for our people.

One of the first people Chaplain Pagano discovered in crisis was a young woman. When the chaplain asked her how she was doing, she just shrugged her shoulders. Eventually, she confided she was facing bitter marriage problems. Chaplain Pagano learned her husband also worked in the factory, but he worked in a different area. He went to the man and found him glumly packing wiper motors. As Chaplain Pagano began talking to this man, the husband admitted he had been abusive to his wife and was sorry for what he had done. He felt, however, that his wife wouldn't forgive him.

Before the week was over, Chaplain Pagano had helped the couple reconcile. Both the husband and wife forgave each other and both began to exhibit renewed energy for their jobs. They became model employees in attendance, quality, and productivity. Appreciation for our chaplain in the factory began to grow.

Later, the young husband who had been helped told me, "You know, this place has done something for me. In the places where I have worked in the past, no one cared about me. All they were interested in was how much work I could do. Here, I feel like a valuable person, like someone really cares."

His words were the validation we needed. Since then, we have never second-guessed having a chaplaincy program, even though outside consultants have suggested we drop our chaplains and their programs in order to reduce our costs. Instead, we got rid of the consultants!

As the months passed, we heard more stories about marriages being reconciled, work problems being solved, and personal lives being changed. Care from the chaplain was a very real expression that the leaders of the company really did *care* for every Factory Family Member. Working together, Chaplain Pagano and leadership helped employees overcome financial difficulties, personal dilemmas, and family problems, ranging from rebellious teenagers to drug use. We have discovered the more we care for employees the more they care about our business and their work. Our business indicators relating to people, productivity, and quality all improved as we carefully invested in providing chaplains for our growing business.

As we grew, we saw the need for additional chaplains. Most of our chaplains speak multiple languages. As a whole, these languages cover the mosaic of people from many nations and cultures that compose our Factory Family. The positive impact we have is not only on our five thousand employees, but also their spouses, families, extended families, and friends. Our exponential sphere of influence for good is far reaching.

In addition to "counseling" work, our chaplains help employees with needs, visit hospitalized employees, and if employees develop an extended illness, our chaplains keep in touch with them. Connecting with our employees at critical family times, such as births and deaths, has been valuable. Through the years the initial roles of our chaplains have expanded.

WHAT DOES A FACTORY "SPIRITUAL LIFE DEPARTMENT" DO?

As our company grew, we realized we needed to be more intentional and organized if we were going to stay connected with our employees, continue to build trust, meet the needs in a growing workforce, and have the positive people and improved business impact we desired. So we created and funded a department called "Spiritual Life." It is a department that includes our chaplains and has an annual budget, a strategic plan with measurable goals, and a long list of recurring activities. Perhaps, most importantly, our Spiritual Life Department addresses needs in a workforce that has approximately sixty nationalities, speaks more than three dozen languages, and embraces a variety of religious traditions and belief systems that is truly global in nature.

PROGRAMS AND SERVICES DESIGNED TO BE EFFECTIVE

The Spiritual Life Department at CARDONE oversees tailored programs to meet our employees' most important needs, including our chapels and the Care Fund described in other chapters of this book. In addition, the department organizes athletic activities for our employees. It provides special recognition gifts to employees when they marry or have a baby. It also provides company-wide leadership in organizing drives to help the less fortunate during holiday times or special relief efforts, like the one we conducted for those affected by Hurricane Katrina.

Most of the work done by the chaplains is one-to-one individualized service. If you asked a chaplain what kinds of activities have filled his hours during the past week, he might tell you:

- I helped an employee with poor English skills make a phone call to a utility company.
- I counseled an employee about situations that were threatening to break up his family.
- I visited an employee in a hospital.
- I helped a family make plans for a funeral.
- I prayed with a mother whose son had joined the Marines.
- I listened to a man express concern about a problem his teenage daughter was facing and networked him with a faith-based community crisis center.

- I encouraged an employee to excel in his work performance and then seek promotion.
- I spoke with leadership and a new employee about how to have the right understanding about quality workmanship.
- I made a home visit to one of our female employees who is experiencing a problematic pregnancy.

Not long ago, one of our chaplains helped a young woman get to the root of a serious medical problem by going with her to a clinic to help her secure the additional lab tests she urgently needed. The tests revealed a serious problem, which could have caused her death had there been no medical intervention. On another occasion, a chaplain was sent on a mission trip to take funds and supplies to the area from which he had emigrated after the region was hit by a violent storm.

As you can see, the work of our chaplains is diverse. They are always caring and ready to help people solve their problems.

When people think about a "spiritual life" program, they often seem to think that such a department offers only spiritual counseling or prayer. We take a different approach. It is not what we say but what we *do* for people that matters most. One of the greatest roles for this department is to help people network with a wide variety of resources outside the company, including civic, charitable, and even government agencies that have programs and resources to help people in need. Our Spiritual Life Team works closely with the Human Resources and Benefits Department to see who might need additional assistance in connecting with community health providers, government agencies, or groups that specialize in helping with child-related problems at area schools. We are working constantly to network with dozens of agencies, parachurch organizations, counseling centers, and other organizations across a broad spectrum.

Incorporating Spirituality

These are among the better-known organizations and associations available to help business leaders incorporate spirituality into their companies:

- National Institute of Business and Industrial Chaplains
- Marketplace Ministries
- Corporate Chaplains of America
- The Association for Spirit at Work
- The International Coalition of Workplace Ministries

Our chaplains have a thick binder of information formally titled "Chaplain's Referral Resource." This binder functions as an extensive catalog of needs, as well as the services, contact names, and contact numbers for addressing those needs. This reference tool has literally hundreds of referral contacts related to a wide variety of needs, ranging from issues related to divorce and child custody to charitable agencies that will help our workers fill out their income tax forms, to agencies that help people make family budgets. We have been amazed at the effective assistance that already exists within our community. Identifying those who can help and connecting our people to those services is just as valuable as our company attempting to give that service to our Factory Family. Whenever possible, our chaplains link with appropriate community organizations and with family-service care agencies to secure tangible assistance for our Factory Family Members in need.

Finally, it is important to note we ask our chaplains to keep active records about the ways in which they spend their time. Our records reveal there are twenty-five areas of service provided by our chaplains. In any given year, our chaplains are engaged in more than forty thousand personal or key contacts with our employees.

ADDRESSING KEY EMPLOYEE ISSUES

We openly recognize at CARDONE that these six employee issues have huge potential for draining a company's profits:

- Quality
- Productivity
- Morale
- Absenteeism and tardiness
- Safety
- Retention

We ask our corporate chaplains to directly impact each of these six areas by serving the "whole life" of our Factory Family Members. We know if an employee can come to work with a minimal amount of home-related, life-related stress, that employee is going to have a brighter emotional outlook (better for morale), have a clearer mind (directly related to quality, productivity, and safety), and have a greater willingness to work with diligence and develop as a person (related to absenteeism, tardiness, and retention).

ABSENTEEISM AND TARDINESS

A study on "Absenteeism and the Bottom Line" states that 64 percent of unplanned absences are not related to sickness but to employees struggling with unresolved personal issues, including:

- Family Issues—22 percent
- Personal Needs—18 percent
- Entitlement Mentality—13 percent
- Stress—11 percent[1]

Absenteeism and tardiness is often a sign of an *internal* struggle in a person's life. The threat of losing one's job doesn't solve the source of the problem a person may have. It only adds to the internal struggle or stress level in that person's life. Showing care and concern, rooted in value and respect for the person, do work.

Our chaplains follow up on absentee employees daily, making telephone calls to them and, when appropriate, making a personal visit to an employee's home. When needed, they step up to offer assistance with larger life issues.

ASSIMILATION INTO AMERICAN SOCIETY

Philadelphia is a melting pot for many different nationalities. The mosaic of our employees all working productively together is amazing. Through the years our chaplains have provided a great deal of assistance in helping new immigrants assimilate into

American society. Translation is a vital service our chaplains provide. In many cases, our chaplains engage in what we call "culture coaching" to help new employees assimilate not only into the CARDONE corporate culture, but also into life where they live. They have assisted in premarital and marriage counseling, adoption cases, grief counseling, child-abuse cases, and supply food, clothing, and shelter in crisis situations. On occasion, they have performed weddings and funerals.

You may be saying, "Aren't these issues a worker's priest, pastor, or rabbi should address?" Perhaps you are correct, but there are studies that estimate more than 70 percent of American workers have no contact with a priest, rabbi, minister, or imam to whom they can turn in times of need.

By no means are we seeking to replace a person's church, synagogue, or mosque. What we want to provide is a caring environment while at work that includes all our Factory Family.

> *"There is no law requiring a workplace to be a religion-free zone."*
> —JAY SEKULOW, *CHRISTIAN RIGHTS IN THE WORKPLACE*

There are some problems far too complex for our chaplains to address. These are usually in areas such as domestic violence, crisis management, depression, anger management, and long-term problem resolution. In those cases we offer our employees free short-term, voluntary, professional psychological counseling at no charge, a "health" benefit that is above and beyond federal-law requirements. Our Employee Assistance Program (EAP) is just another way we demonstrate our concern for our employees' entire lives beyond the time and problems that they may incur while at work.

REAL GOALS AND REAL RESULTS

We link real business goals with our chaplains' objectives. Two of those goals are related to turnover/retention and absenteeism/tardiness. Our chaplains have strategies, goals, and key indicators for measuring their impact on our people indicators. As an example, in one recent year, the chaplains' annual report revealed that they impacted our business financially in these ways:

- 98 cases of potential terminations were reversed, saving our company $735,000.[2]
- 6,999 cases of potential absenteeism/tardiness were eliminated, saving the company $417,345.[3]

In these two vital areas alone the role of our chaplains amounted to more than $1.1 million in annual cost savings.

A GROWING TREND

We certainly do not believe what we are doing with chaplains at CARDONE is unique. Not long ago the Houston-based National Institute of Business and Industrial Chaplains, an organization representing workplace ministers, priests, rabbis, and laypeople, estimates there are nearly four thousand trained and certified workplace chaplains in businesses across our nation. Strong chaplaincy programs exist in companies such as Pilgrim's Pride and Tyson Foods (the two largest poultry-producing companies in the world), McKibbon Hotel Properties (a management firm that trains its leaders to serve others), McKinney Aerospace (which services large and small jets), and McLane Pacific (a wholesale distribution center serving the western United States).

There's an old adage that says: "The time has come and now is." I believe that is true for the role of chaplains in the workplace. More than ever the time for workplace chaplains is now!

QUESTIONS ONLY YOU CAN ANSWER

1. Would chaplains benefit your organization? In what ways?
2. If you had chaplains in your business, what would be their job description?
3. What measurements would assure you of a chaplain's benefit or effectiveness?

14

A Job Description Rooted in Caring

Taking on the Problems That Come to Work with Your Employees

When a person comes to work, he brings his entire self. A person doesn't leave his or her family concerns or personal problems at home when he walks out his front door and heads for work. When an employee goes to work leaving a family member at home ill or in the hospital, that situation rests in the heart and mind of the employee all day. There's no shelving of that concern from nine to five. If a person is financially overwhelmed, the stress of that problem continues to churn inside the person. There is no "turning off" the personal stress at the company door.

A policy of "park your personal problems at the door" is unrealistic. A person simply cannot compartmentalize his life like that and, in my opinion, should not be asked to do so. We are all creatures who have emotions, experience problems, and have needs. Rather than seeing a person only as a "skill set" applied to a task, we see a person as a whole human being.

Very often it is not laziness or lack of motivation that causes a worker to be tardy or absent. Rather, it's often a matter of transportation, child-care, or health-related issues. If those matters can be resolved, the worker not only shows up on time but works with better productivity, higher quality attentiveness, and more safely. Those who are helped often become more loyal to the employer who has helped them. Their job satisfaction skyrockets. Team morale rises and employees are more likely to become helpful to others on their team. Over all, the work environment improves and the business is recognized as a great place to work.

> *"I recently learned the Hebrew word* avodah *is the root word in the Old Testament for two English words:* work *and* worship! *I like that. Work is not a curse. We worship God through our work."*
>
> —Michael Cardone Jr.

On the other hand, if an employee's personal matters cannot be resolved, a person's productivity, efficiency, and quality of job performance will be impacted and the company suffers right along with the employee.

At CARDONE, we not only recognize that people show up at work with personal problems, but we actively attempt to help them work through their problems. The primary job description for our chaplains is for them to be corporate culture bearers: to be caregivers to our people. When this is done properly, both the person and our business benefit.

While people can change, they often need help making positive changes. Our servant leaders work effectively with their people to encourage, develop, and promote them, but there are occasions when a chaplain is able to bring the extra energy needed to unlock the potential in a person in a way the immediate workplace leader cannot. Our chaplains act as a safety net for our leaders, "catching" people who may be "falling." When a leader sees a person with a need and connects him with a chaplain, oftentimes positive things happen for the leader and the employee. That's good for the business too.

THE MARKS OF A GOOD CHAPLAIN

There are several traits we look for and seek to develop and encourage in our CARDONE chaplains.

1. Identification with the Factory Family

Our chaplains are trained individuals, with practical ministry skills, but their foremost qualification is their genuine love for people. When we need a chaplain, we initially look within our business for someone who has a good reputation with people. We look for persons who are committed, hardworking, and openly promote our corporate culture and values. The majority of our chaplains have worked within our operation and proved themselves. They are respected as bridge builders, negotiators, and peacemakers within our Factory Family.

2. Good Samaritans and FireFighters

Our chaplains see themselves as "good Samaritans," a term related to a parable Jesus told about a man from Samaria who, in a very practical way, helped a needy person who had been robbed and beaten. When a worker comes to a chaplain on a Friday and says he and his family will be evicted from their house tomorrow, he doesn't need a sermon or a prayer. He needs someone who will organize coworkers to store his furniture, find a house or hotel where the family can stay the weekend, and then help them find a new place to live on Monday. Prayer is good and quoting Scripture is valuable, but when a person and his family are standing on the curb, they need someone to care in practical ways. That is true compassion. That is what Jesus would do, and that is what our chaplains are all about.

3. A Willingness to Be Available 24/7

One of our chaplains said, "Sometimes we might be compared to firefighters, because we have to be ready at all times. Whenever the bell goes off and a need arises, we have to be ready." While chaplains work normal shift hours, they are also called to be available to employees 24/7. In other words, they are always "on call."

Our chaplains reach out to our people beyond normal workday hours and beyond company walls. The goal is to build *relationships* and to establish trust. At times, a person will need a friendly face showing up in a hospital waiting room, help with translation, transportation after hours, or a friend to help intervene in a family crisis. Chaplains are involved in recruitment and hiring, and they often are the ones who introduce new workers to their fellow employees.

4. Prayer

Our chaplains believe in prayer and they are confident and willing to pray for our employees, if requested. When someone is in need, that person is usually open to having someone pray. Very few have ever said, "Do not pray for me."

5. Respect for Religious Diversity

As S. Truett Cathy of Chick-fil-A has noted, "There are no Christian companies, only Christian people." We are a company with Servant Leadership and decidedly biblical values. That means we care about our people enough to get involved. It does not mean, however, that we require all of our employees to be Christians. Nor do we actively engage in proselytizing. At the core of all our policies is this simple mandate: care for and meet people's needs.

The United States of America has laws related to religious freedom, which require a much greater sensitivity to the way people conduct business. Arguments about the role of religion in public life fill our airwaves, courtrooms, and also the agendas of Congress and the Supreme Court.

In recent years we have seen numerous heated debates around the world related to "religious tolerance." I am all for tolerance, not because I can't make up my mind about what I believe, but because I see it as the only way we can truly work together as people of diverse religions and faith-related beliefs. CARDONE employees are of all walks of life, faiths, persuasions, and religions. I respect their right to believe and worship in the way they choose. They also respect my right as a private business owner to promote the values in which I believe strongly. In all cases, it is my responsibility to make certain that no employee is kept from practicing his or her own faith and also to make certain that differences in religion don't interfere or impact the work we do.

"Too often we underestimate the power of a touch, a smile, a kind word, a listening ear, an honest compliment, or the smallest act of caring, all of which have the potential to turn a life around."[1]

—Leo Buscaglia

Our workers are guaranteed freedom of faith under law. I do not seek to convert others to my beliefs with words. But I do seek to model my beliefs openly and to express what I believe when and if I am asked.

Legally, many of the issues of faith in the workplace are covered under Title VII of the Civil Rights Act of 1964 and governed by the Workplace Religious Freedom Act of 2003.

At CARDONE we have adopted these general policies:

Don't Hire or Fire Based on Religion. We do not ask questions about religious views during our interviews related to hiring. Religion has no bearing on whether a person is hired or fired, nor does it impact whether a person is promoted.

Live Out Your Faith, but Don't Force It on Others. Trying to pressure people to embrace beliefs is not only wrong, it is bad for business and it is bad for faith!

Love in Action. I believe Christians should be known for their love and what they *do* for people, not what they *say* to people and certainly not for using pressure tactics. Just as it is important to know and obey the laws of the land, it is equally important to remember the biblical command to "love one another" (1 John 4:7) and to practice the Golden Rule, which says, "Do unto others as you would have them do unto you." Put yourself in the other person's shoes. Is what you are conveying true care and concern? Will the person see that you sincerely care about them? If not, don't do it. What is important to God is not ideology, but people. God did not create religions; people did. The religions of people are rooted in rules and convey the idea one can work or earn their way to God by obedience to a set of rules. God is not into religion. He is seeking a relationship with us. When that happens, like God, we will care rightly about people. People, God's creation, are the commodity of heaven.

AN ONGOING CHALLENGE

Legal counsel will normally advise against trying to include faith in the workplace. HR departments may also discourage such activity to avoid potential lawsuits. At CARDONE we know it is possible for people to express spirituality in the workplace, if they do so in ways that build up people, bring people together, and make the workplace better. Biblical principles can be lived out in ways that respect the dignity and freedom of all people, regardless of their beliefs.

PUTTING SPIRITUALITY IN CORPORATE OPERATIONS

We believe people have a spiritual dimension. Having chaplains available to the people in our workforce is one of the ways we acknowledge and address the spiritual aspect of people's lives.

We certainly aren't the only company that is acknowledging spirituality in the workplace. The November 1, 1999, issue of *Business Week* noted a spiritual revival is sweeping across corporate America. Gone is the old taboo against talking about God and spirituality at work. The article states, "With more people becoming open about their spirituality—95 percent of Americans say they believe in God . . . and 48 percent say they talked about their faith at work that day according to the Gallup Organization—it would make sense that, along with their briefcases and laptops, people would start bringing their faith to work."

In the July 9, 2001, issue of *Fortune* magazine, Marc Gunther wrote, "God and Business: Bringing spirituality into the workplace violates the old idea that faith and fortune don't mix. But a groundswell of believers is breaching the last taboo in corporate America." This article further underscores the revival of spirituality in the business world.

An "interest" or "awareness" of spirituality in the workplace, however, isn't the same as having an operational plan for infusing spiritual values into the core of a company. At CARDONE, we want our employees to be very comfortable expressing their personal spiritual values through their work and in their relationships with one another. And, we want them to be comfortable with engaging in behaviors that reflect a positive, moral, family-oriented value system.

We aren't a church.

We aren't a social services agency.

We aren't a hospital or a rehabilitation center.

We are a competitive business based upon biblical principles and values, which are reflected by our actions in the workplace and through our performance in the marketplace. At CARDONE Industries we want our people to be comfortable in expressing their faith by how well they work with each other, our customers, and our suppliers.

Heroes with Problems

People often refer to various characters of the Bible as "heroes" of the faith. Are you aware of how many well-known biblical heroes had huge problems? The next time one of the people you supervise seems to be more trouble than he is worth, reflect on the following Bible personalities and the challenges they faced . . . and overcame.

- Noah was a drunk.
- Abraham was old.
- Joseph was a "dreamer."
- Jacob was a liar.
- Joseph was abused.
- Moses stuttered.
- Gideon was afraid.
- Samson was a womanizer.
- Rahab was a prostitute.
- Timothy was too young.
- David had an affair.
- Elijah was suicidal.
- Isaiah preached naked.
- David was a murderer.
- Jonah ran from God.
- Naomi was a widow.
- Job went bankrupt.
- John the Baptist didn't know how to dress.
- Peter denied Jesus as the Christ.
- Jesus' closest followers fell asleep while praying.
- Martha was a worrier.
- Zechariah didn't believe an angel and was struck dumb.
- Mary Magdalene once had seven demons.
- The Samaritan woman was divorced more than once.
- Zacchaeus was short.
- Paul was too religious.
- Timothy had an ulcer.
- . . . And . . . Lazarus was *dead*![2]

QUESTIONS ONLY YOU CAN ANSWER

1. Does your company ask employees to leave their personal problems in the parking lot? Is that approach working successfully?
2. Does your company acknowledge or address the spirituality of your employees? If so, in what ways?

15

Crossroads: The Intersection of Faith and Work

An Exciting Venue for Sharing Life's Challenges

As we began to develop the chaplains in our plants, we recognized certain employees were starting to seek out quiet places to meditate during nonworking times. In response to this, we built a chapel in Plant Number 1. In the following months, the idea of a designated "chapel space" had become so popular we opened chapels in various other plants. The chapel spaces were, and still are, made available to Factory Family Members before work begins and during lunch hour breaks.

In February 1980 Dr. Norman Vincent Peale came to dedicate the chapels located within our factories. He said, "I can pick up the Spirit of the Lord when I come into a place and it is here in this plant." *We* certainly believed that, but it was good to hear a highly respected and notable person confirm our feelings.

The chapel-meeting programs have taken various forms through the years. About the only constant has been *music*! Almost from the beginning, employee choirs and bands formed to take part in the chapel meetings. The overall employee involvement at chapel meetings has consistently reflected a diverse blend of ethnicities, nationalities, cultures, and languages. It's amazing the music a multicultural, multinational group can create!

MEETING AT THE "CROSSROADS"

We call our chapel meetings before work "Crossroads," indicating a time when faith and work interact and intersect. The meetings are voluntary, on-site, and take place weekly in one of our conference rooms (we call them "Decision Rooms"), chapel facilities, or right on the factory floor.

> *"And don't just do the minimum that will get you by. Do your best. Work from the heart for your real Master, for God."*
>
> —Colossians 3:22–23 msg

The chapel services are planned and led by employees. Our goal is to have people attend not because they feel obligated to attend but because they want to attend.

Does everybody attend chapel services? Not everyone attends, but I am convinced even those who don't attend know and appreciate our company leaders, who are serious about living out our commitment to honor God in all we do. Providing chapels is another way we have attempted to bring spirituality into our corporate operations.

Several principles successfully guiding our corporate chapel meetings are:

Honor God First and Foremost

Chapel meetings support our overarching corporate objective to honor God in all we do. Our chapel meetings inspire people to link their faith in God with their work. They provide opportunities to express our faith-based corporate values. Regardless of who and how many attend, chapel meetings make the statement that God is honored in our business through all we do.

I see my role as creating an "environment" in which chapel services and prayer can take place freely and voluntarily beyond normal work hours. Since our chapel times are employee developed and run, I don't lead the meetings and rarely speak in them.

Respect People's Free Will

We believe God created human beings with the freedom to choose what they believe and how they will act upon those beliefs. It is not our place as a company to impose religious views, but we can and do attempt to model them through our caring for people.

Seek Engagement

Chapel isn't a place where our leadership brings lectures. It's a place where people from many areas of the company gather to express their journey, their faith, and how they and their area of the business seek excellence in honoring God. Through the years we have discovered a vast reservoir of talent in our company, including speaking and musical talent.

Crossroads chapels have addressed many different topics. For example, we have had chapel services that focused on modeling "Servant Leadership." Another theme was "Knowing Your Neighbor," which focused on learning from the people we work beside and sometimes barely know. "Ministry of Business" chapel meetings have reflected on how to integrate faith and work. "Faith-in-Action" chapels have spotlighted employees who volunteer and give back to the community.

MAKE MUSIC TOGETHER

Music is a universal language and we encourage our employees to use the language of music in our chapel meetings. I have been astonished at the number of people in our company who, with their musical talent, willingly participate in our chapels.

MAKE IT REAL

Many of our themes for chapel meetings are related to special times of the year. Family values and roles are usually a part of the chapel meetings near Father's Day and Mother's Day. We recognize the National Day of Prayer with our own event. We celebrate Memorial Day with a special ceremony honoring employees or their family members who have served or are serving in the military. We also celebrate Martin Luther King Day, Fourth of July, and Thanksgiving. At Easter we have a cast of twenty employees who present an Easter drama. This drama troupe "travels" to all our plants during lunchtime the week before Easter. Christmas choirs and concerts have showcased the amazing variety and amount of musical talent that exists in our company.

MAKE IT RELEVANT TO THE WORKPLACE

Typically, the annual chapel schedule includes outside speakers, government officials, customers, suppliers, company leaders, and various employees. Meetings may include interviews, round-table discussions and/or video teachings, or talks that focus on issues pertaining to faith in the workplace and God at work.

ENCOURAGE AND INSPIRE

Our chapel meetings are encouraging and inspiring. Part of our emphasis on encouragement involves promoting a caring spirit and community service. We also recognize Factory Family Members who model outstanding volunteerism in the community with the "Excellence in Ministry" award.

MIX IT UP

Our company is incredibly diverse and we want our chapel meetings to reflect this diversity. From time to time, we put the focus of a chapel service on a particular ethnicity or culture. A variety of outside speakers, whose very presence in our operation is motivating and encouraging, have included leaders such as Norman Vincent Peale, Charles Stanley, Robert H. Schuller, and D. James Kennedy. We have also featured sports legends such as the late Reggie White (NFL Eagles and Packers) and David Robinson (NBA San Antonio Spurs). These leaders are examples and role models who are known for integrating their faith and work.

AN EXCITING VENUE!

Time and again, those who visit us and attend our chapel meetings are moved by seeing people of various socioeconomic and ethnic backgrounds come together to express their faith in word and music. Frankly, I am moved too.

QUESTIONS ONLY YOU CAN ANSWER

1. Is there an appropriate time and place for the people in your company to share their faith?
2. How might a group meeting that relates faith to work enhance your corporate values, company morale, or your employees' needs for significance?

16

Exceeding Customer Expectations

Building Relationships Through Excellent Service

I once saw a sign at a customer service desk that said, "Due to the unusual number of customer service calls we have temporarily closed the Customer Service Desk." How can a customer service person care about customers if the company leadership hasn't demonstrated it cares about the worker put in charge of customer service? In his bestseller *The 7 Habits of Highly Effective People,* Stephen Covey says, "Always treat your employees exactly as you want them to treat your best customers."

Our dedicated customer-service people have learned to agree with the customer, until the customer agrees with you. They are trained to be "fix it" oriented. When a customer has a problem, they don't focus on why or who messed up. Instead, they focus on what we can do to make it right.

> *"The customer is the foundation of a business and keeps it in existence."*
>
> Peter Drucker, *The Practice of Management*

It seems to me that most customer service organizations could function more effectively if they worked on fixing and solving problems rather than arguing about who is right or wrong. I have found that when we are willing to accept responsibility for a problem, regardless of who caused it, the customer's anger is often diffused and we are on our way to finding a solution and satisfying our customer. While there have been a few who abuse our good practice, we haven't changed our approach of doing whatever it takes to solve the problem.

WHAT EVERY CUSTOMER WANTS FROM US

What is it that our customers request and expect? Their expectations are usually couched in these four questions:

- Can I get the part I need from CARDONE?
- When will I get it?
- How much will it cost?
- When I get it, can I be confident it will work?

These questions bring us to the issues of Order Fill and Parts Performance.

> *"People hear with their eyes before they hear with their ears."*
>
> —Michael Cardone Jr.

ORDER FILL

At CARDONE we remanufacture and catalog more than forty thousand specific part numbers, offering full coverage for all makes and models of cars and light trucks from 1920 to current model years. Every year that list of part numbers grows. These part numbers or SKUs are in our catalogs and on our shelves for immediate delivery. Our parts service the 270 million vehicles on the road in the U.S. and 300 million in Europe. When a car owner goes to a repair shop for the windshield wiper motor on his 1967 Thunderbird or a brake caliper for his 2007 Lexus, he wants the part *now* and he wants his car back on the road today, not tomorrow.

Having the right part in the right place is the essence of our business. The remarkable distribution system of the independent aftermarket allows repair shops in most cities across America to find the parts they need in their city and have them delivered to the repair shop or car owner within twenty minutes. This is the strong value proposition of the independent aftermarket and it is why selling automotive parts via the Internet has not impacted our business significantly. The continued viability of this distribution system depends, however, on a never-ending flow of automotive parts from the manufacturer or remanufacturer to distributors and local auto parts stores so they can get the parts to the repair shops, which install the part on the vehicle.

We make it our goal to achieve the highest order fill rate possible. I'm proud to say our order fill rate has always been one of the highest in our industry. This requires an enormous investment in planning models, tooling, equipment, and inventory. Most of all, *high order fill* is who we are and it has been a CARDONE distinctive for years. As one of our major customers said to me, "Just keep shipping those good parts and we will be a customer for a long time." It sounds simple, but in today's world of personalized vehicles, alternative fuels, and propulsion systems such as hybrids and diesels, it is becoming increasingly difficult to meet the challenge of order fill in the same ways. We are faced with what we call a "parts proliferation tsunami." This requires us to be working continually to find new and faster ways of getting parts to the customer when he needs them, and remanufacturing has the fastest and most effective business model to accomplish this.

PARTS THAT FIT AND FUNCTION EVERY TIME

When a vehicle is down, the customer wants it fixed "yesterday." Cars and trucks are vital to our busy lives and people will neither wait for slow service nor tolerate poor quality.

We have addressed this by investing heavily in high-tech equipment for our remanufacturing processes, which gives us consistent high-quality parts that are equal to or better than new. Our test equipment simulates on-car, road-tested performance with stress requirements for our parts. That investment in technology continues to rise as more car parts use integrated circuits and have more complicated designs.

NOT BRAGGING—JUST THE FACTS!

This rise in integrated circuits, control modules, and onboard computers had a profound impact on the aftermarket industry. Some found it too costly to invest in the technology necessary to remanufacture these newer and more complex parts. We decided to invest in the best people and high-tech equipment to enable us to supply the finest and most complete line of electronic parts in the aftermarket.

Today, the average age of vehicles on the road is nearly ten years. Have you ever tried to purchase a component for a 10-year-old computer? It's virtually impossible, but by our remanufacturing process of electronic automotive components, we provide parts that keep cars and trucks operating and on the road for decades.

> *"Over the past four decades we at* CARDONE *have received numerous major awards related to customer satisfaction, and it comes from* CARDONE*'s effort to always try to do what is right."*
> —PETER CALO JR., CARDONE EVP OF SALES

Over the years, we have kept pace with the demanding qualifications of a variety of international automotive quality certifications, including ISO, QS9000, and TS16949. That means we meet the international standard to supply automotive products globally for the original equipment manufacturers as well as the automotive aftermarket.

As stated previously, our mission is to be the best *remanufacturer* and supplier of automotive parts in the world. There are five basic steps in the remanufacturing process:

1. Disassembly
2. Cleaning
3. Repair and replacement of all worn or damaged parts
4. Assembly
5. Testing and packaging

The parts we remanufacture go through our demanding fivefold proven processes that assure our parts are of equal or better quality than the original equipment parts. We have the advantage of seeing the flaws in the original manufacturers' design, and we correct those design errors in our remanufacturing processes.

We work to be the best supplier in our industry. Even though we have been recognized with many "Top Vendor of the Year" awards from our customers, this does not satisfy us. Nor do we see those awards as any type of guarantee a customer will continue to do business with us. We must continue to get it right inside, personally and in our business, to compete and continue to win in the marketplace. We know our only job security is a satisfied customer. We sum it up this way:

Under-Promise and Over-Deliver

CARING FOR OUR CUSTOMERS

At CARDONE our customers are not only the millions of automobile and truck owners around the world, but also the people who work for companies such as NAPA, AutoZone, CARQUEST, Pep Boys, O'Reilly Auto Parts, Advance Auto Parts, Auto Value, Bumper to Bumper, Federated, Original Equipment Manufacturers, and many other companies distributing our products. Many of our parts are sold under the CARDONE brand, but most of our auto parts are sold under our customers' own store brand. So, in effect, this means there is a CARDONE part in virtually every auto parts store in the U.S.

One of the best definitions of customer service I have ever heard came not from a business book or lecture, but from our director of customer advocacy, the person who heads up our customer service department at CARDONE. Larry stated it best when he said:

> Customer service is doing the things you do, not because you have to, but because you *get* to. At home, I'll put the

> dishes in the sink or the dishwasher, not because my wife expects me to, but that's how I express my love for her. It's the same for what we do for customers. We don't feel as if it is an obligation. It is a joy.

We have spent a great deal of time and energy developing a corporate culture that places high value on customer service, and I am encouraged when I hear statements like that. His comments signal our values are permeating the entire organization. It is even more exciting for me to hear of examples that tell me we are putting our values into action.

> *"There is a realization throughout the company that the customer signs our paycheck. If we don't keep the customer happy, we are not going to get a paycheck at some point in the near future. So, we work to keep our customers happy. The customer is the boss."*
>
> —TIM SPULER, CARDONE
> EXECUTIVE VP OF GLOBAL OPERATIONS

Here, on the East Coast, we occasionally have those "Nor'easter" winter storms, which start with a few flurries and end in a full-fledged blizzard. No storm, however, was going to keep a couple of our sales veterans from keeping their appointment with the president of a national network of warehouse distributors.

Here's the way I heard the story.

> We started our drive to the Baltimore Airport early in the morning, and the snow was already coming down. By the time we got to the airport, four inches of snow were already on the ground with more snow on the way. The

> airport was closed, so we talked back and forth about what we were going to do. We considered turning around, but agreed together to keep the appointment. So, that's what we did. We drove for seven hours through the most severe snowstorm we ever drove through in our lives. We got there within a half hour of the appointment, and nobody there could believe what we had done. I'm sure some of them even thought we were crazy. But they were also impressed with our commitment. We told them we were going to be there and we kept our word.

The story might have ended there, but it didn't. Some time later this group inducted our VP of Sales, Peter Calo, into their "Vendor Hall of Fame."

Did one crazy drive through a blizzard win that award? No, but it was the first step in a series of events that demonstrated our commitment to our customers.

Our people are committed to what we do and see themselves as an important part of our corporate culture. How do I know that? They tell me so and our customers confirm what they say. I am honored to work with such great people and I value their contributions and commitment.

Committed employees are best developed within a company that has a corporate culture rooted in values. I strongly believe:

The best customer service is value based
and rooted in Servant Leadership.

Strong values and a desire to exhibit Servant Leadership can't help but spill over to the way a person treats customers. Everything related to quality products, order fill, and responding to customer requests with urgency springs from a corporate culture that places a premium on people, performance, and excellence. Certainly, from a faith perspective, "doing unto others as you would have them do unto you" has direct customer-service applications!

HELPING CUSTOMERS GROW THEIR BUSINESS

We are not reactionary to our customers only when they ask or have a problem. Our goal is to work proactively with our customers to help grow their businesses. We know if we can help our customers resolve their business problems and grow their businesses, we will also grow. Doing the right things for the right reasons reaps long-term relationships and rewards.

I am a huge fan of growth. Growth is a good thing and a sign of a healthy business. I am continually looking for growth at CARDONE. If there's an area where we are not growing, we need to figure out why not. If our customers aren't growing their businesses, we want to do anything we can to help them. As they grow, we grow with them.

BASIC PRINCIPLES FOR CUSTOMER SERVICE

The basic principles we at CARDONE believe are vital to excellent customer service lead us to:

- Look for ways to make it easier for customers to do business with us.

- Give customers the best value.
- Build long-term relationships.

We have no doubt that an enduring relationship *will* be profitable for us in the long term, especially if it is rooted in doing the right things for the customer.

A SATISFACTION OF WANT

Peter Drucker said *consumerism* demands that "business define its goal as the satisfaction of customer needs."[1] I continually ask, "Are our customers *satisfied?* Are they truly getting what they *want?*" These inquiries go beyond the question, "Does the customer like what he gets?" Our customers want:

- Quality products
- High order fill
- Fast and reliable delivery
- Competitive and fair pricing
- Commitment to attentive service

If we are the best at what we do, we will have a customer for life.

QUESTIONS ONLY YOU CAN ANSWER

1. How do you define customer service?
2. Do your customers trust you? What is your company doing to win and maintain trust?

3. If you and your company are pursuing *good* but not *best* when it comes to customer service, what would it take for you to pursue *best*?
4. How do your customers define quality? Have you taken the time to ask them?
5. What are you doing to raise the bar on your own personal performance level of excellence when it comes to customer service?
6. How do you respond to the phrase "under-promise and over-deliver"?

17

A Company That Gives

Making a Difference Inside and Outside

I am proud to be an American. We are the most giving nation on this earth. Americans give billions of dollars every year to thousands of worthwhile charities and causes around the world.

CARDONE is a company that gives. We have a heritage of giving to our Factory Family Members, to charities, and to the communities in which we are located. As I grew up, I saw generosity, graciousness, and giving modeled by my parents. My father was a giver from his earliest years. He had a compassionate heart and was quick to do whatever he could, with whatever he had, to help those he encountered with genuine needs.

Early in my father's life he was walking home from work one night when he came across a man named Mr. Grundini—a grouchy old hermit, who could often be seen hunched over the railroad tracks picking up stray pieces of coal and putting them in a gunnysack. My father often stopped to help Mr. Grundini gather up a few pieces of coal and, occasionally, he made sure that a full bag of coal was left on Mr. Grundini's porch so he could heat his tiny house.

Years later, Mr. Grundini caught up with my father on the street and held out a simple gift, a hammer he had used for years in his work as an itinerant carpenter.

"No, Mr. Grundini, I can't take this," my father said.

"Sí, sí," said the old man. "You good boy. Take it with you."

> *"Organizations are not just places where people have jobs; they are neighborhoods, our communities. They are where we join with other people to make a difference for ourselves and others. If we think of them only as the places where we have jobs, we not only lose the opportunity for meaning, but we endanger the planet. It is in . . . organizations . . . and among friends that you spend your time, pursue your most pressing purposes, and find meaning in your life."*[1]
>
> —Keith H. Hammonds, *Fast Company*

My father had that hammer until the day he died. It served as a powerful symbol to him that a gift *always* has impact, even if you don't see the impact with your own eyes.

Through the years, we have given 10 percent of our net profits, either through the CARDONE Foundation or directly from the company.

THE CARDONE FOUNDATION

My parents established the CARDONE Foundation in 1977, and Jacquie, my wife, now serves as the president of the foundation. She established a board of trustees in 1998 to oversee the foundation's work. Since then we have become a family foundation. All of our children and their spouses are involved. Our son Ryan serves as the Program Director and leads with a passion. Our commitment is to give to organizations that are truly making a demonstrable difference in people's lives. Our mission is, Impacting Christ's kingdom through the ministry of business. This clear mission, along with the foundation's guidelines and processes, narrows the focus of our giving.

We focus our giving on organizations in Philadelphia and in other areas where we have operations. We want to impact organizations that are reaching out and making a difference in the lives of the people who are in our own workplace neighborhoods. We also look for local organizations meeting the needs of our employees, including social, financial, physical, medical, addiction-related, or other family needs.

We make grants to nearly three hundred organizations every year. These include schools, churches, parachurch organizations, humanitarian organizations, and groups involved in relief efforts for victims of tragedies.

We have several guidelines for our giving:

1. We give to IRS-approved 501(c)(3) organizations.
2. When making a grant, we do not give to a general operating budget, since this has the potential of creating dependency.
3. We direct our giving to a specific project within an organization and not to the general fund.
4. We require independent references and a full application process.
5. We give to organizations where our businesses are located.
6. An organization is only eligible for funds every three years.
7. We are a granting foundation and do not engage in managing the projects or organizations to which we give.

INVOLVING OUR EMPLOYEES IN OUR GIVING

How do we decide which grants to give? Some of the grants are determined by the Foundation board and a portion of the grants are determined by our own employees, through their participation in our "Employee Giving Program." Rather than insisting the Cardone family or the Foundation's board members make all the decisions about what is given to whom, we empower our leaders to direct a portion of our giving. We believe our employees have great insights into where we can make the biggest impact in our greater community.

Our Basic Business Philosophy and Practice

Good business goes far beyond status and profit for a few. CARDONE exists to realize a profit, which impacts the lives of many. We commit our business to the mutual benefit of its owners, employees, customers, and communities. Our profits are reinvested back into the business, its people, and its communities.

Here's how this program works. Every year hundreds of our leaders participate in the Employee Giving Program. All participants recommend their choice of a qualified 501(c)(3) charity for a CARDONE Foundation grant.

The Foundation responds with a letter and grant check to the charitable organizations, stating a Factory Family Member has selected the organization and that we are giving in recognition of the leader's contribution to our business.

Over the years our Employee Giving Program has helped hundreds of small local organizations, as well as national and international organizations, including the American Cancer Society, American Diabetes Association, Girl Scouts of America, National Multiple Sclerosis Society, Salvation Army, World Vision, and the YMCA. Some of the giving has also gone to faith-based works that represent a wide variety of churches and organizations.

The Employee Giving Program has become part of our Triple Bottom Line goal of having social impact as a company. It is also a means of creating a feeling of genuine significance and engagement within our leaders as they see the fruit of their labor having an enlarged impact in supporting organizations that are important to them. When our employees participate in these philanthropic efforts, we have found they share a renewed sense of purpose for their work at CARDONE and this has been a key component in building our corporate culture of shared values.

THE CARDONE CARE FUND

In addition to giving "outside" our factory walls, we have a program called the CARDONE Care Fund for helping our own Factory Family Members.

This fund is administered through our chaplains to meet the temporary, emergency needs of our Factory Family. Each year, approximately 8 percent of our Factory Family Members, or more than three hundred people, receive assistance from the Care Fund to help them in a special time of financial or material crisis. In one case, we purchased an airline ticket so that a worker might attend her mother's funeral in her home nation. In another case, we helped a family who had faced a crisis by paying directly to the electric company a backlogged bill just before their electricity was to be turned off. Employees who are victims of house fires, automobile accidents, robberies, and other unexpected tragedies benefit from this fund.

This fund is designed to assist CARDONE employees in unusual circumstances after all efforts have been taken to obtain assistance from other sources. In giving these grants, we first investigate the need to assure that it meets the guidelines of the program. The grants are not given to meet routine obligations, nor are they given if a need can be covered through other benefit programs.

> *"A giving company creates giving employees who create a giving culture."*
> —Michael Cardone Jr.

What is the source of money for this fund? The funds are raised at our Annual Charity Golf Outing and come from our many excellent suppliers. Years ago we established a policy with our suppliers asking them to not make gifts to our purchasing people. Our thinking was and is: *Why should just a few benefit when all of the Factory Family Members deserve to be recognized and rewarded?* Also, giving to the employees making purchasing decisions can create an obligation that does not fit our definition of conducting business with integrity. Instead of "insider giving," we challenged our suppliers to contribute to our Care Fund, which benefits *all* in our Factory Family. We explained the Care Fund's purpose and guidelines. Today, our suppliers of goods and services contribute annually and take satisfaction in knowing the positive impact their giving is having on many people, for which we are grateful.

To qualify for a Care Fund grant, an employee or leader initiates a formal request. The chaplain and the employee's leader agree that this is a bona fide need and apply preestablished guidelines to determine the amount we can give. In most cases the Care Fund check is not made out to the employee, but rather to a service provider, such as a funeral home, airline, electric company, gas company, and so forth. The result is we are able to help hundreds of our people in a time of crisis and we believe that is the right thing to do. Our employees are grateful we care enough to give tangible help.

A NEW INITIATIVE IN HEALTH CARE

CARDONE recently joined forces with Holy Redeemer Health Systems to create the "Holy Redeemer Family Health Center at Cardone," which is located on our property. The 2,500-square-foot facility offers CARDONE's employees and their family members primary health care, internal medicine, care management, and diagnostic and wellness services, with maternity and pediatric care envisioned for the future. Holy Redeemer staff members, including physicians and nurse practitioners, provide the health care services in a holistic manner.

This health care facility is located within minutes of our main headquarters and five other plant locations. The Center offers flexible hours to give our employees a good alternative for their nonemergency health care needs. In addition to the services provided at the new Center, our Factory Family Members have access to Holy Redeemer's entire health system.

From our perspective, this is an example of what can happen

when organizations with very different missions find common ground. As far as I know, this is an innovative program for business. I firmly believe, however, faith-based health care makes a difference. Since we are a faith-based business, this seems to be a natural fit and an extension of our overall goals. The new Center gives people access to help meet their physical and emotional needs, and there are people available to offer prayer, if desired. The Center's focus is on providing quality health care and wellness.

QUESTIONS ONLY YOU CAN ANSWER

1. How does your organization give back to the communities in which you work?
2. Do you have a means of involving your employees in your corporate giving?

18

Cultivating Servant Leadership

Adopting a Corporate Leadership Style

At CARDONE, we have taken what I believe is a step beyond the establishment of corporate values. We have identified and incorporated a leadership model that is congruent with our corporate and family values. In addition, we expect our employees to use our corporate values as the guidelines for their behaviors while at work.

The same is true for our approach to leadership. Our "Servant Leadership" model is the framework for the leadership behavior that influences our people at all levels in the business.

A CONSCIOUS AND INTENTIONAL DECISION TO BE A SERVANT LEADER

When I became CEO of CARDONE, I faced a decision about what type of leadership model and style I would embrace. The world of business offers many different leadership styles, approaches, and models. Thousands of books and seminars have been published or produced about leadership. But which leadership models work best and achieve lasting results? That was a question I grappled with personally.

In reflecting back over the last thirty years, I believe two of the most valuable leadership lessons I learned did not come from business books, periodicals, or seminars. One of the lessons I learned from my father. Dad summarized his leadership philosophy in six simple words: "The fish stinks from the head."

I can't begin to tell you how many times our family has referred to those words of wisdom. The meaning is clear. Leadership is responsible. What you see at the bottom of an organization is what comes from the top. I cannot expect any more of my organization than I expect of myself. I set the standards with my behaviors. "Do what I say and not what I do" does not work.

> *"Whoever desires to become great among you, let him be your servant."*
> —MATTHEW 20:26

Jesus, who was the Master, Teacher, and Leader, illustrated the second valuable leadership lesson I learned. He washed His disciples' feet as a servant and taught leaders to serve one another and others. This style of Servant Leadership transformed His followers and, in turn, they embodied His message and passed it on to others. This principle was foundational in our leadership from the early days of our business but was not yet formalized. Management experts have come to call this leadership style "Servant Leadership." I determined that Servant Leadership would be the bedrock of our company's leadership philosophy and practice. It has positively impacted my family, life, and business.

In the 1970s, one of the best-selling business books was *Looking*

Out for #1. Today, that book has been largely forgotten. Although the Bible was written thousands of years ago, it is still in print. The New Testament—and specifically the four Gospels—is a history of the greatest leader this world has ever known. If you are a leader who likes to read books on leadership, try reading the New Testament as a book on leadership!

Robert Greenleaf wrote in his book *The Servant As Leader:*

> We are beginning to see that traditional autocratic and hierarchical modes of leadership are slowly yielding to a newer model—one that attempts to simultaneously enhance the personal growth of workers and improve the quality and caring of our many institutions through a combination of teamwork and community, personal involvement in decision-making, and ethical and caring behavior. This emerging approach to leadership and service is called servant leadership.

David Gergen, who worked for five U.S. presidents (Ford, Carter, Reagan, Bush Sr., and Clinton), was quoted in a *U.S. News & World Report* article as saying Servant Leadership is "taking hold in high-performing organizations." He also said, "Increasingly, the best leaders are those who don't order but persuade; don't dictate but draw out; don't squeeze but grow the people around them."[1]

At CARDONE, we have found the Servant Leadership model creates the culture that enables us to best achieve our corporate objectives and goals. The following model graphically depicts the difference between Servant Leadership and the customary traditional leadership model followed in many organizations.[2]

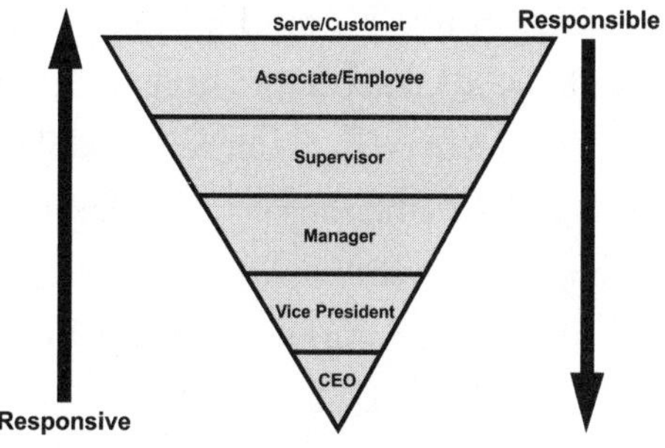

Servant Leadership Model

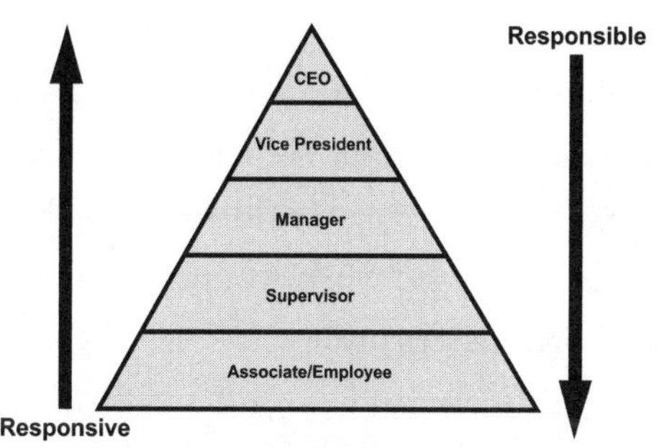

Traditional Leadership Model

I frequently talk to our leaders about Servant Leadership. I strive to model it in all my dealings with employees, customers, suppliers and, most importantly, my family.

Not long ago, Paul, an up-and-coming leader at CARDONE was promoted to lead a large division of our company. He didn't begin his leadership of this team by calling everybody together to dictate or talk to them about how he intended to manage the division. Instead, he rolled up his sleeves and began to work alongside his workers on the production line. This not only helped him develop relationships with his workers, but it gave him a familiarity with the production process he never could have gained by staying in his office and giving orders. He quickly began increasing morale in his area. Before long, efficiency improvements became the norm. This leader has moved on to even greater responsibility in our company. His example and the efficiency results achieved are typical of those who are using the Servant Leadership model. These are precisely the leadership results we need in today's hypercompetitive market.

NOT EVERYONE IS WILLING TO SERVE

In a 2004 Gallup Study of more than one million employees, the number one reason people quit is their boss. Fifty percent of the employees surveyed said they would fire their boss. Their final finding was that poorly led work groups are 50 percent less productive and 44 percent less profitable.

> *"Organizations led by servant leaders are more likely to take better care of their relationships to customers and colleagues. Today, if you don't take care of your customers, somebody else is waiting, ready, and willing to do it. The only thing your competition can't duplicate is the relationship your people have with your customers."*
>
> —KEN BLANCHARD, CUSTOMER MANIA!

So much of business success hinges on effective leadership. I believe a key reason for unsuccessful leadership is every person with the task or ability to lead is not willing to serve. For some, serving is a concept that runs contrary to personal desires for power, ego, or pride. In such cases, the person likely has his own agenda and is not willing to sacrifice it for the goals of the organization. For others, a failure to serve is likely linked to a perceived need to "perform at all costs." And in still other cases, the "end justifies the means" to such an extent that his leadership ability is compromised. I have encountered leaders who produced results but destroyed people in the process. The Servant Leadership model in contrast is balanced and is a means of producing extraordinary results while building positive relationships.

I certainly understand the need to *perform*. The intense competition we experience in our global market puts a tremendous amount of pressure on our business. Throughout our industry, I see leaders feeling pressure to meet short-range performance goals. This leads many to put their own priorities before the organization's goals. In recent years we have seen loud-and-clear examples of this at Enron, Tyco, and World Com.

A few years ago, we had a leader with great potential. He was performing with results, but there were problems with his leadership. I became increasingly concerned when other leaders found it difficult to work with him. He wasn't building relationships, but rather, he was consumed with his personal goals and performance. Over time his responsibility grew, with many people reporting to him, but he was not a servant leader. Rather than confront him about his leadership style, I initially ignored the warning signals and focused on other, more positive results.

THE TRAITS OF SERVANT LEADERS

To serve the people of CARDONE, leaders are expected to exhibit the following traits:

- Appreciate and respect diversity
- Tolerate mistakes
- Support and respect the family institution
- Develop successors
- Listen to their people
- Communicate business information to their people
- Anticipate and respond to the needs of their people
- Model and encourage continuous improvement
- Mentor people and help them develop

I have found that a servant leader will make himself accountable first to God and then to others. When leaders want to control, dominate, and protect their power and position, they are either insecure, in over their head, or don't have their ego under control.

Ken Blanchard and Phil Hodges wrote in their book *The Servant Leader,*

> One of the quickest ways you can tell the difference between a servant leader and a self-serving leader is how they handle feedback, because one of the biggest fears that self-serving leaders have is to lose their position. Self-serving leaders spend most of their time protecting their status . . . they think your feedback means that you don't want their leadership anymore. Servant leaders, however, look at leadership as an act of service. They embrace and welcome feedback as a source of useful information on how they can provide better service.[3]

When I talk with former employees, they are usually quick to comment how special their working years at CARDONE were, primarily because of the corporate culture in which we work. I greatly attribute that atmosphere to Servant Leadership.

SERVANT LEADERS VS. SELF-SERVING LEADERS

There are a number of traits that clearly differentiate servant leaders from self-serving leaders. For quick comparison I have noted these differences in the following chart.

Servant Leaders	Self-Serving Leaders
Willingly seek feedback or suggestions	Protect their status and don't want feedback or suggestions
Desire to train and plan for succession	Addicted to power and recognition, and are afraid of loss of position and power; do not want to face replacement
Share credit	Desire to receive all credit
Humble	Boastful
Promote others	Promote self
Challenged and motivated by change	Fear loss and resist change

Which type of leader do *you* want to follow? To me, that is the key question to ask about leadership. The kind of leader you would most like to follow is the kind of leader you should seek to be.

QUESTIONS ONLY YOU CAN ANSWER

1. How do you describe your leadership model?
2. Are there concrete and practical ways you might *better* serve the people with whom you work?
3. Is the leadership model you follow compatible with your company's culture?

19

The Seven Choices Servant Leaders Make

Servant Leadership Is a Growing, Learning Process

All of us are born self-serving creatures. To be a servant leader goes counter to our human nature. To pursue Servant Leadership seriously, a person must first determine this is the best model for his or her leadership and then commit to follow this model diligently and consistently over time. Servant Leadership requires ongoing effort to experience ongoing growth and results.

Because we believe so strongly in Servant Leadership, through determination and commitment we developed a training program called "Leadership 101: An Introduction to Servant Leadership," which we require all our leaders to take. One of the persons who really contributed and led our internal effort of teaching, modeling, and enhancing Servant Leadership culture at CARDONE Industries is Jim Comenzo. He developed great material that we have used extensively. In the following few pages, you'll find an overview of the program's lessons, which focus on the seven key choices a servant leader must make.

CHOICE #1: SERVANT LEADERS CHOOSE TO LISTEN

Many workplace problems begin because someone doesn't listen. Our goal is to have everyone listening to everyone else. If a person develops this life skill, he will be able to resolve problems better and faster, because he has made the attempt to understand the other person's perspective on an issue.

It seems as if listening would be one of the easiest skills to develop, but it is actually one of the most difficult. Our ego is the biggest obstacle to listening; we would all rather listen to ourselves talk than to listen to someone else. The cardinal rules of listening, however, are these:

- Don't interrupt. *Just listen.*
- Don't make judgments. *Just listen.*
- Don't make suggestions. *Just listen.*
- The focus is on the other person, *not you.*

The key rules for responding after listening thoroughly are these:

- Repeat back to the person what he has just said to make sure you heard him and that he knows you understood him.
- Be open and honest. If you don't understand what the person is saying, admit it. Say candidly, "I don't understand. Please help me understand."
- Seek better understanding by asking additional questions, such as, "Why do you feel this way?"
- Stay positive. If a person makes negative comments, find a

way of repeating the meaning of those comments back to the person in positive language.

- Address the issue. Do not blame or belittle the person who brings the issue to you.

Listening is a *choice*. When a person makes the choice to listen, he is on his way to being a servant leader.

CHOICE #2: SERVANT LEADERS CHOOSE TO EMPOWER OTHERS

If you put the focus on yourself—your needs, your ego, your agenda—more than on the needs of others, the people you lead will not have an opportunity to grow, learn, and develop.

Why empower others? Very simply, no one person can do as much or as well as a team who work together with united focus toward a common goal.

> *"Leadership is anytime you are trying to influence the thoughts and actions of another individual in either your personal or professional life."*[1]
>
> —PHIL HODGES

Insecurity is one of the main causes for people to fail in becoming servant leaders. The insecure person is afraid others are going to make him look bad, take power away from him, or gain advantage over him. Insecurity causes our natural human response of self-preservation to kick in, with attempts to protect power and position. When a person insists on solving everyone's problems and making all the decisions, that person is generally reflecting insecurity.

Servant leaders look at problems and issues as an opportunity to help others grow. They aren't afraid of helping other people develop and become leaders, even though some of the people they help may rise higher in the organization than they will. Servant leaders understand one of the responsibilities of a leader is to empower and develop people.

We regard Servant Leadership as the single most important principle in the *total* organizational development of our company. If an organization is filled with serving leaders, that organization is going to be developing people at all levels, at all times. The overall atmosphere is one in which development and growth is the norm. On the other hand, if an organization is filled with leaders who don't want to share what they know, because they don't want others to rise higher than their rung on the corporate ladder, that organization will be stunted. People led by self-serving leaders will be discouraged and may leave the company, and the people who are not developing people will not be able to rise higher in the organization, because they haven't trained their replacements.

Throughout my career, I realized developing people would be the limiting factor for the growth of our company. Therefore, in our leadership training we teach a two-part process:

- Servant leaders are required to have regularly scheduled, one-on-one meetings with their people. This is a key component of Ken Blanchard's Situational Leadership training done at CARDONE. I realized what a powerful tool this can be in developing people, leadership, and an organization.
- Servant leaders are to have regular team meetings with those they lead, with well-thought-out agendas for each meeting.

Once again, the purpose of both these meetings is to keep the channels of communication open and to value people.

CHOICE #3: SERVANT LEADERS CHOOSE TO HAVE A POSITIVE ATTITUDE

Most people would rather work for a positive, supportive boss than one who has a negative attitude toward life. Unfortunately, many people never get a choice about what kind of person they work for!

It has been proven that a quality leader has a positive impact on the productivity of those he leads. Think about a time in your own past when you worked for a positive, supportive leader. Using a scale of one to ten, with ten being the best, how would you rate your productivity during that time? Now, using the same scale, recall your worst leader and rate your productivity during that period. The difference is likely to be significant! Spend a few moments recalling how much *more* productive you could have been during the time you had a poor, unsupportive, or negative leader.

Leadership impacts every part of a triple bottom line. At times, a person in leadership may have a legitimate reason for being negative. At CARDONE, every leader is encouraged to *learn* how to deal with his own attitude and to become an expert in handling both praise and criticism. Having a positive attitude means even criticism and conflict can be handled in a context of hope and helpfulness. We encourage our leaders to:

- Care how you come across; be intentional about the messages and impressions you are sending; recognize that your words and the way you express your thoughts have an impact on the emotions of those with whom you work.

- Create and maintain a sense of urgency that keeps people and projects moving in a positive direction.
- Demonstrate a belief in yourself and in all the members of your team.
- Give the credit for success to others; accept responsibility for failures without blaming others.

CHOICE #4: SERVANT LEADERS CHOOSE TO HEAR HONEST FEEDBACK

We have lines of authority that we respect in our business, but we do not want lines of communication that limit people from being free to speak, offer ideas, and give feedback at any level. By its very definition, feedback is a two-way street. If we make our customers happy, we want to spread that good news around so everyone in the company can enjoy the feeling of a job well done. If we fail to make our customers happy, we also share that information. Honest feedback should travel throughout an organization in all directions, not just from the top down. Servant Leadership is rooted in the concept that honest feedback, when given in the right spirit and attitude, is the best way to develop people and the organization.

We offer this five-point test to assess whether a leader desires honest feedback:

1. Do you listen, or do you interrupt?
2. Do you inquire, or do you blame others?

3. Do you seek understanding, or do you make excuses?
4. Do you ask for suggestions, or do you defend yourself?
5. Do you accept feedback as a gift, or do you change the subject?

You may never have asked yourself such questions, but your employees already know the answers about you!

CHOICE #5: SERVANT LEADERS CHOOSE TO SOLVE PROBLEMS QUICKLY

In the movie *Speed*, starring Sandra Bullock and Keanu Reeves, a busload of passengers is trapped in a bus that is transporting a deadly bomb. As the clock on the bomb edges closer and closer to detonation, a crazy criminal, played by Dennis Hopper makes increasingly outlandish threats and demands. Sometimes, in any given business day, it may seem as if there are numerous ticking bombs about to go off and you are in charge or are the only one who can save the day!

At CARDONE, we want leaders who will surface, not hide, issues and then work with urgency to get the problem resolved. We do not expect leaders to have all the answers, but we do expect them to know the problem. As a leader there is nothing wrong in saying, "I don't have the answer, but I will find someone who does and get back to you." When people see that a leader is willing to "escalate" an issue to the highest level of the business until an answer is found, the people have greater respect for their leader and are willing to offer their best efforts and creativity in finding a solution to the problem.

Our natural tendency seems to be to avoid or deny problems, rather than to confront them. Perhaps we do this out of fear of having to deal with the emotions a problem may be generating, but remember, nothing is resolved if problems are not addressed. We teach our leaders a six-step process for addressing problems.

A = Admit there is an issue and take ownership.

B = Begin immediately to address the problem with urgency.

C = Communicate up the chain of command until the problem is resolved.

D = Develop a plan of action.

E = Engage your team.

F = Follow up and give feedback to the people responsible for exposing the problem.

We teach our leaders to face problems head-on. The longer people put things off, the bigger a problem grows and the more devastating it can become.

We recognize that behind every problem is a person, either an employee or a customer, who is not getting what he or she needs. Servant Leadership sees resolving issues as an opportunity to serve, further develop, and build relationships. We may not be able to fully give a person all he needs, but we can listen to the situation and attempt to provide as much as possible. Sometimes, the right answer is saying "no," and in those cases, it is just as important as saying "yes." But the most important thing is to let people know you care by listening to them.

CHOICE #6: SERVANT LEADERS CHOOSE TO LEAD WITH RESOLVE

Good intentions don't get a person very far in the business world. Action is what speaks and what solves problems. Our Servant Leadership training stresses leading with a resolve to *act* in a way that gets results. We teach these five steps:

- Commit from the outset to follow through; if you say you are going to get something done, get it done!
- Always seek to find a better way.
- Stand up for, and do, what is right, even though it seems difficult at times.
- Recognize that every problem has an *opportunity* embedded within it.
- Understand that successful problem solving involves urgency, persistence, and resolve.

When dealing with a problem, put a fix in place as soon as possible. Then, drill down until you get to the root of the problem. As simple as it may sound, clearly defining the problem is the most important step in solving the problem. While the fix is in place, do further research on the causes of the problem and make decisions aimed at resolving those causes *permanently* so future problems are averted. If your decisions don't produce the desired result, admit you made a mistake and make a new and better decision!

Harold Geneen, who wrote three excellent books on business management, clearly points out managers do not need to make every decision correctly in order to be successful overall. If a leader is wrong, he can always correct his mistake. The damage of no decision is worse than making a wrong decision. When in leadership, be confident and make decisions.

CHOICE #7: SERVANT LEADERS CHOOSE TO SERVE

Leading by serving doesn't make a person weak, indecisive, or trapped by a desire to be loved by everyone. Rather, leading by serving means you lead with *trust* rather than intimidation. You seek to influence rather than rule. It means you lead people and focus on the greater good of others, the entire team, and the business, rather than seek your own personal good.

Humility is a key characteristic of a servant leader. Every person has an ego. We are born with it. Ego is part of our humanity. People who learn how to manage their egos are the people we want to promote at CARDONE. Humility usually isn't a trait promoted in most business books, but it is the vital element in the Servant Leadership that Jesus Christ modeled. We view humility as the "secret key" that unlocks all other elements of the Servant Leadership model. Serving with humility means:

- You serve others first, not yourself.
- You serve both internal and external customers.
- You place the needs of others before your own.

AN ONGOING JOURNEY

I don't claim in the least to have arrived at a perfect place in Servant Leadership at CARDONE. I further recognize the development of Servant Leadership is an ongoing journey in my personal life, in the personal lives of our leaders, and in our company as a whole. Our intent and motivation toward becoming servant leaders will help us develop the quality and lasting results we need in today's hypercompetitive market.

QUESTIONS ONLY YOU CAN ANSWER

1. Which of the seven Servant Leadership choices have you made personally?
2. Which of these choices is most problematic for you?
3. In which areas do you feel the most need for personal growth and change?
4. How will you go about making these changes?

20

Recipients of a Legacy . . . and Passing It On

Standing on Tall Shoulders

My father, Michael Cardone Sr., was not a man who dreamed small. He was a risk taker, who dreamed big and had boundless faith in a loving God. In his mid-fifties, when many businesspeople are starting to think more about retirement than new business ventures, my father left a successful family business he founded to launch a new company.

My father's life was a dramatic rags-to-riches story, the kind you read about in novels or see in movies. He grew up in a coal miner's family. His small physical stature did not suit mining. One day, he volunteered to mine coal just to get enough to heat his family's church. At the end of a day, when he discovered he had barely mined enough coal to heat the church for one day, he gave up all thoughts of becoming a miner and sought a different life. He set out to build his new life during the Great Depression, when work was scarce. Eventually, he found a job at an automotive repair shop.

He first began to remanufacture automobile fuel pumps in the basement of his grandmother's house in Philadelphia. He dealt with each fuel pump one by one, by hand. From that humble beginning, he went on to start several automotive parts remanufacturing businesses.

For many years my father dreamed I would work in business alongside him, we would build a great company together and I would take over the business one day and take it to greater heights. In his book *Never Too Late*, my father wrote, "Ever since Michael Junior was born, I dreamed of the two of us sharing a partnership in the remanufacturing business."

There was only one main obstacle in the way. Dad and his brothers were in a company together and their company policy stated that no one's son or daughter could become an owner.

The only way for us to be in business together was for my father to sell his ownership in the company to his four brothers, resign as president, leave that company, and start his own business. The departure was amicable, and my father committed not to compete. That was a major and risky business challenge for him, but it was a risk he was willing to take. In 1970, at age fifty-five, my father founded CARDONE. I was a senior in college at the time.

A Fast-Moving and Very Clever Mouse

In 2000, the Wharton School of Business awarded CARDONE Industries its annual "Family Business of the Year Award" for a large company. Wharton cited three main factors:

- A strong and demonstrable linkage between our family values and our business culture
- Our contributions to both the Philadelphia community and the automotive industry

- The involvement of multiple generations of family members in our company, something that has been proven difficult in many other family-owned businesses

The Philadelphia Business Journal interviewed me about the award and I said this: "The family has given us an edge. The larger companies are getting bigger, and we've had to become more responsive to the customer to stay in business. I like being the mouse running between the elephant's toes."

I wasn't as certain about our business future as my father was, but I knew several things with certainty. I loved cars. I loved to work and be active physically. I also knew I enjoyed a factory operation, because a factory is always busy. I knew I loved taking things apart and putting them back together.

At age eleven, I was the youngest person to enroll in and complete the A.C. Delco Carburetor Repair and Service Training Course at the General Motors Training Center. When I was only six years old, Dad removed a small carburetor from a Briggs & Stratton two-horsepower gas engine, and at our kitchen table, he taught me to disassemble it, clean its parts, and replace the worn parts with new ones. I loved the challenge. That remanufactured carburetor from an old lawnmower sat on my parents' bookshelf for decades and it is now in my office.

As a youngster and teenager, I worked in my father's remanufacturing business during my vacation breaks from school. And, I knew as a recently married young man, I needed a job after I graduated from college. My wife, Jacquie, and I prayed about going into business with my father and felt confident this was God's plan. So, following graduation, we returned to Philadelphia and began to work at Dad's side.

Those early days are amazing to recall. As a filing system for the business, my mother cut openings in several shoeboxes and labeled them "invoice," "statements," and "bills." After I graduated and we moved to Philadelphia, Jacquie took over the bookkeeping. Mom helped with inventory control and customer orders. Dad scouted out and purchased the old used parts, the "cores," which are our basic raw material.

One of the things families can do better than just about any other institution is pass on values to the next generation, and my father worked hard at that all his life. I spent many great years working alongside my father and learning from him.

That is not to say working with my father was easy. Far from it! We had different personalities, grew up under different family and social conditions, and had very different ideas. It took me years to learn how to make suggestions to my father without his regarding my suggestions as confrontational. If I erred during those years, it was probably in my overeagerness to put into motion my own ideas about what would grow the company.

SIX LESSONS I LEARNED FROM DAD

Through it all, however, the lessons I learned from my father were invaluable, and I fully intend to pass them on to the best of my ability. There were six key things I learned from Dad that remain invaluable to me to this day.

1. Roll Up Your Own Sleeves

One of the things my father taught me is leaders should never think of themselves as being too "big" or too "important" to roll up their sleeves and plunge into things. He often told me, "You should never ask anyone to do something you wouldn't do yourself."

2. Stay on Top of Your Game

I learned to continue learning, stay prepared, and believe there is no finish line. I can never know too much about my business. Therefore, I should keep on top of things, know what is going on, and give attention to critical detail. My father was always interested in the latest and most up-to-date methods. He was always looking for a better way and I am that way too.

I remember seeing a photo of Olympic track star Michael Johnson crouched in the starting blocks, waiting for the gun to sound. It looked as if each and every muscle on his body had been trained and disciplined through relentless study and practice for this one moment. Like a professional athlete, I want to have that approach to my business, my chosen "sport." I want to see each new day as the moment for which all other days have prepared me.

I love golf, so I study the work ethic of great golfers such as Tiger Woods. Tiger Woods may look laid back, but he is usually out on a golf course every morning at five o'clock, perfecting his swing. He focuses on the details of his work and rolls up his sleeves to push himself to the next level time and time again. I am keenly aware there is *always* more to learn, and as I learn more, I become capable of taking my company to its next level.

Dad taught me to know more about my business than anyone else knows. "That's the key," he said. "No one will take your business from you if you know more about it than anyone else, especially your competition."

3. Give It Your All

My father never did anything halfheartedly. He focused on the task before him and gave it his best.

A few years ago I was privileged to play a round of golf with the great Arnold Palmer. Palmer was in his seventies at the time, but he certainly was not "settling down." I witnessed his fiercely competitive nature emerge on the hole in which I was fortunate to hit my drive five yards farther than he did. He did not like the thought of somebody besting him, because for him, golf was not a "game." It was his life. Even when he was playing with an amateur like me, Palmer was playing like the professional he was! He still made all his shots as if he was playing in the Masters Tournament.

4. Respect Every Person

My father treated everybody who worked for him as if they were part of our family. He wanted the best for everyone and was willing to ask for, and listen to, advice from others. He never thought too highly of himself. There was no discrimination and no regarding "us" and "them."

Whether American-born or immigrant, factory worker or manager, my father believed everybody was created equal in God's sight; we just have different jobs. He did not regard his job as being more "important" than anybody else's. Only that his job was *different*.

Dad's respect for other people was a part of his faith. He believed strongly in the Christian concept of loving one's neighbor as one's self, and he expanded that to include all people, regardless of their background. He saw all people as God's children, and therefore, worthy of dignity and respect, and I totally agree with that perspective.

5. Pay Attention to Details

On more than one occasion, my father told me, not only by his words but also by his deeds, the secret of a business' ongoing success is found in the way a company deals with details. In short, *everything* matters.

The result of believing and then acting upon your belief that every customer matters, every employee matters, and every problem matters is an atmosphere of caring. When leadership cares, employees care, customer needs are met, employee concerns are addressed, problems are seen as opportunities to get better, and as long as we are in business, continuous improvement will be our daily routine.

6. Stick to the Fundamentals

I became president of CARDONE in 1988, and in 1994 my father died. At first, I tried to lead the business as my father had. I thought I had to replace him. My father was a pioneering entrepreneur, but that just didn't fit my makeup. I read about a young leader who tried ruling twice as hard as his father. In the end, he lost the respect of his employees. I did not want that to happen to me.

Like any leader, I had my own ideas about how I wanted to do things differently. I finally realized God made me a different person than my father, and just as God made my father for a special purpose and time, He had made me the person He needed me to be. I am trying to teach my son, Michael, this same principle. He is now in the business and I know that God has made him the way he is for *his* time and the fulfillment of God's purpose in *his* life.

I began to research and study the trends and predictions about where our business was headed and what would be required in order for us to stay in business. I saw our customers consolidating and made the decision we would grow with our customers and become a big supplier to big customers. To remain a small business with small customers in one location would be certain death for our company. My father had taught me all opportunity comes from God, and as I look back, I believe my seeing the opportunity for growth was the "defining moment" in my career and for our business. I chose to grow and become a big supplier to big customers.

Over time, I instituted a number of changes. Most of them had to do with advances in technology and methodology. I can honestly say, however, that I didn't have to change *any* of the fundamental principles that guided this business from day one. That's because those principles were based on unchanging sources of wisdom and truth. The values on which our company is based aren't Dad's values alone. They are God's ways and timeless values found in the Bible.

The powerful thing about biblical principles and values is that they always apply to life and business. Certainly no one person can grasp all of them or perfectly apply them to all life's challenges, but with God's help and working with a team of committed people who believe God's principles, I have been able to apply God's truth to our business. If I can, you can.

A FAMILY BUSINESS: GOOD OR BAD IDEA?

To some people, when they hear of a "family business," they envision a small "mom-and-pop shop." While there may be hundreds of thousands of such small businesses across the United States, there are also many large and prosperous family-controlled enterprises, a third of which make up the Fortune 500. Some of the best-known companies in our nation are family-controlled, including Ford Motor Company, Wal-Mart, Cargill, Anheuser-Busch, and Perdue Farms chicken. According to family business expert Mike McGrann of Babson College, which is one of the nation's leading institutions on family enterprise, there are more than twenty million family-owned businesses in America.[1] Furthermore, according to a 2003 *Business Week* article, 60 percent of publicly traded firms in the U.S. are family controlled.[2]

> *"I believe the strongest and most meaningful motivators are not necessarily the materialistic, but the intangible. In this respect, there is perhaps no better carrot than approval from someone you truly respect, whose recognition you seek. Acknowledgement, a pat on the back, a wink, a nod of recognition or praise from someone you hold in high esteem is . . . the most valuable carrot of all."*
>
> —Coach John Wooden, Wooden on Leadership

I have had occasions to talk with a number of family-controlled-business leaders, as well as those who have studied family businesses. Some owners believe family businesses face huge competitive disadvantages, determining they will not be able to compete with large publicly held companies. On the contrary, while I attended the Wharton School of Business Family Business Program, I learned that they regard family-owned-and-operated businesses as having a competitive *advantage*. Decision making is faster and for the long term, not just the next quarter. Customers, suppliers, and employees are treated personally and with greater care, and because of this there are higher levels of loyalty, commitment, and dedication in family businesses.

Over the years, I have seen competitors come and go. I have seen family-owned remanufacturing businesses go public, in private equity roll ups, and I have seen larger national companies fail while trying to function and compete in our industry. On paper these competing companies appeared to be well positioned to take away a significant share of our customer base, and in a few cases, for a time, they did take some of our customers. But over time, these former family businesses lost the personal touch and their attention to detail. They became impersonal and financially focused on their shareholders, rather than their customers. In time these businesses have not survived.

In one case, a former family-owned, now publicly traded competitor, offered products at a dramatically lower price and they "bought" a lot of business. It seemed the approach worked. But, the lower prices the company offered were achieved by cutting corners on quality, product availability, and customer service. The customers, who changed over to them, eventually balked and came back to us, and the competitor filed for bankruptcy.

Certainly, I am not claiming CARDONE has survived these various competitor challenges because we are family-owned. Rather, I am stating our family ownership, along with other important business factors, has helped contribute to our continuing success.

THE "FAMILINESS" ADVANTAGE

A few years ago, we hosted a team of scholarly researchers from Babson College in Wellesley, Massachusetts, and Widener

University in Chester, Pennsylvania. The team of Timothy G. Habbershon, Michael N. McGrann, and Mary L. Williams were testing the thesis that family businesses have competitive advantages over other companies. They had heard about our unique business culture and they wanted to know more. We invited them to check us out and conduct interviews with our people. The resulting paper was a powerful portrayal of what they called "the familiness advantage."

Among the advantages of "familiness" cited in their report and other similar reports are these strengths:

- An ability to make changes very quickly
- An ability to model and implement values that create a strong and unified corporate culture
- An ability to initiate and support "causes," with full recognition that cause-oriented companies are the vanguard of success in today's business world
- A strong ability to implement succession plans without a disruption of company values or business momentum

All of these advantages are ones we have experienced and continue to experience at CARDONE. Part of what makes "familiness" work at CARDONE is our core value of treating *all* of our employees as Factory Family Members. Part of what makes "familiness" continue to work at CARDONE is the fact that we also have third-generation leadership in our company who are committed to our mission, objectives, and values. There is unity and cohesiveness across generations that provide sustainability for our culture and ongoing business strength.

QUESTIONS ONLY YOU CAN ANSWER

1. Identify a leader you admire. What do you admire most about this leader?
2. Is there anything you might do to create a "family culture" and reap some of the advantages?
3. If you are a small company, how might you use your size as an *advantage* to compete effectively against larger companies?

21

Define Yourself, Define Your Company

Embrace Your Own Abilities and Keep Developing Them

What comes to mind when you think of the word *creative*?

An artist, like Picasso?

A composer, like Tchaikovsky?

Do you think of *yourself*?

How does your creativity express itself? What do you create? How do you express your creativity? How much latent creativity exists in your organization? How do you encourage and reward creativity in others?

I've read dozens of definitions for creativity and a number of theories about creativity. The way I express creativity is finding solutions to problems.

I am familiar with problems. It seemed like I grew up in the eye of a hurricane of problems. As a child, I didn't like to color within the lines and this was a problem for me, because my teachers interpreted this inclination as either incompetence (an inability to color within the lines) or disobedience (a refusal to color within the lines).

I had other problems in school. As I stated earlier in this book, sixty people were in my senior class and I graduated number fifty-nine. "Hey," I told my parents, "at least I wasn't number sixty!"

My tested IQ revealed I wasn't stupid, but at the same time I wasn't doing well in school. Only recently, as my wife and I worked with a family member on learning difficulties, I discovered I have had Attention Deficit Disorder (ADD) all of my life. On the one hand, it was a relief to have a "reason" for the many problems I encountered in school. On the other hand, I'm frustrated I didn't discover this earlier in life. When I was in school, little was known about ADD, and few had patience with my restless mind, endless curiosity, and creativity.

"What is the next important contribution you can make? How will you build on your remarkable success, and how does that success enable you to do what you could not have done before? How will you use your accumulated wealth of relationships, learning, and experience in order to turn potential into reality? Your task is to convert experience and wisdom into a solid foundation for the future. You have an unprecedented opportunity. Take it seriously."

—PETER DRUCKER, *TRAINING AND DEVELOPMENT JOURNAL*

Even though I didn't earn good grades in elementary school or high school, I had other interests and developed other skills, which made up for my lack of academic achievement. As a boy and teenager, I loved to be active and I still love to be busy. I once begged my parents to allow me to stay extra weeks at a summer camp, because there was so much to do. I had and continue to have a tremendous amount of physical energy. That is also true for many people who have ADHD. A person who has ADD has difficulty focusing or concentrating. ADHD is "Attention Deficit-Hyperactivity Disorder," where a person not only has difficulty focusing, but also has a tremendous amount of physical, pent-up energy.

Through the years, I actually believe I have been able to use what others call a "learning disability" to my advantage. People with ADD are kinetic learners. This means they learn by doing and are challenged by things that are physical in nature. As a young person I was a gymnast. I enjoyed working with my hands. In my college years, I felt God speaking to me very clearly that He was going to give me a ministry that involved working with my hands, not my mouth. I wasn't destined for a career in speaking. I was destined for a career involving kinetic skills, things I can do with my physical being while using my creativity. A manufacturing business suits me perfectly. A book that helped me understand and learn more about this topic is *Driven to Distraction* by Edward M. Hallowell and John J. Ratey. (For additional information on ADD, visit the Web site www.add.org.)

People with ADD usually have a short attention span. I do, but this has led me to challenge people to explain things or express themselves in ways that are crystal clear and concise. I believe this has benefited all of us at CARDONE, not just me. I always ask for the punch line or conclusion of a presentation first. If I don't know where the presentation is going, my mind may wander someplace else before the presentation ends.

> *"Delight yourself also in the LORD, and He shall give you the desires of your heart. Commit your way to the LORD, trust also in Him, and He shall bring it to pass."*
>
> —PSALM 37:4–5

People with ADD often leap from one subject to another. In my experience, the process of going from one topic to another has been conducive to finding new approaches and creative solutions.

Some of the people who have worked with me the longest call me "the idea machine." Certainly, not all of my creative ideas are brilliant, or even workable, but they do inspire additional thought and an ongoing creative process.

One of my gifts is the ability to see options. I periodically engage in intuitive, creative "brain dumps." I have lists of ideas that are beyond anything that can be accomplished in two-dozen lifetimes. If a person discusses a problem with me, I can often come up with many possible approaches to the problem, each of which has potential to work. I tend to say, "Here's a list of things to try; let me know how it turns out." The danger in that is I can get ahead of a process or begin to create something my company is not yet ready to implement.

Fortunately, I am working at CARDONE with people who know how to deal with my creativity. Leaders need to manage down the organizational chart, but they need to manage up the organizational chart too. In many companies, such a list from the CEO would be daunting. Most people want their "leader" to give *one* answer to a question, *one* way of approaching a challenge, or *one* solution to the problem. My leadership style is to help stimulate creativity that will eventually produce answers for solving problems in new and unique ways.

Rather than see my ADD as a hindrance, I regard it as a tremendous asset. I was created with ADD, causing me to think differently than other people. I doubt I would have accomplished all that I have accomplished if I had been given a different learning style or a mind that processed information in another way.

Why share all this with you? Because I encourage you to know yourself, even as you strive to learn all you can in your business. Every person has a unique learning style and emotional intelligence.

I encourage you to discover your learning style, understand your own level of creativity, and then surround yourself with people who will complement your style.

When I put the concepts of leadership and creativity together, I derived the profile for leadership below. This profile both complements and enhances the principles of Servant Leadership.

PROFILE OF THE CREATIVE LEADER

- A creative leader must learn from the past, but be ready to adapt to the future.
- A creative leader should base all business decisions on core values, while seeking fresh and innovative ways to express those values.
- A creative leader acknowledges each person is a unique individual.
- A creative leader addresses each relationship as a one-of-a-kind opportunity to impact another person and inspire that person to perform at his or her optimum ability.
- A creative leader also acknowledges personal weaknesses and imperfections in himself and others. Once admitted, those weaknesses become an opportunity to grow and to develop and, ultimately, to turn a weakness into a strength.
- A creative leader constantly renews the wellsprings of creativity that are found in his or her faith and core values. The leader takes time to reflect upon and feed the creative spirit within and to nourish his or her faith and spiritual values from which all creative solutions flow.

If you aren't personally a very creative person, I strongly encourage you to associate yourself closely with some people who are creative. It takes more than nuts-and-bolts management skills to run a company in today's business climate.

NEVER STOP GROWING AND LEARNING

One of the ideas that arose out of Japan's post–World War II industrial revolution was "continuous improvement." This philosophy encouraged employees throughout a company to improve the way they performed their tasks bit by bit every day. Although it may sound simple, this continuous improvement approach had a profound impact on Japanese companies and, in turn, the world's economy. (As part of a system aimed at continuous improvement, the Japanese solicited and implemented employee suggestions. They called their approach "Kaizen." The Kaizen system fostered Quality Circles in which employees could make suggestions daily for improving quality and productivity.)

> *"The concept of life in business as separate from spiritual life is false . . . Our lives must be considered as one . . . our business life should be affected by the spiritual. If and when a person grasps that truth, they are living right and in truth, and one's business will prosper."*[1]
>
> —Sir John Templeton

I encourage you as a leader or potential leader to adopt the idea of continuous improvement for *yourself*. Get as much input as you can. Study your business and your craft thoroughly. Don't stop studying it, don't stop learning, and don't stop being willing to reinvent yourself. I believe there is always a better way to do something, and there is no end to using your creativity to find solutions.

QUESTIONS ONLY YOU CAN ANSWER

1. What unique abilities do you bring to your job?
2. How do your unique abilities, learning style, and creativity impact your career and company?

22

Two Key Leadership Issues

How Are You Organized? Whom Do You Trust?

Every CEO is invariably confronted with critical issues. Two of them are leadership and trust. What influenced me most on these issues came primarily from personal experience.

My father's leadership style would probably be regarded as "old school" by today's standards. He was hierarchical in his approach and a firm disciplinarian. My father could be loving and compassionate, but he also could be very tough on people whom he believed were not pursuing excellence as urgently as he thought they should. He certainly was not the only business owner of his era who adopted this type of strong, entrepreneurial, top-down leadership style.

I struggled with the fact that my leadership style was different. It was only later in my career that I realized my leadership style was right for taking CARDONE to the next level.

> *"A heart motivated by self-interest looks at the world as a 'give a little, take a lot' proposition. People with hearts motivated by self-interest put their own agenda, safety, status, and gratification ahead of that of those affected by their thoughts and actions."*
>
> —Ken Blanchard and Phil Hodges, *Lead Like Jesus*

My father ran the business like a wagon wheel with himself at the hub. Everyone reported to him and brought issues to him for decisions. This entrepreneurial approach worked well while the business was small and experiencing an extremely high rate of growth as a start-up, but it would not work today with our more than five thousand employees globally. So, I made significant and necessary changes. I adopted an empowered style, which gives clear direction on what we want to accomplish. This challenges our great people to find the best way to accomplish our goals. An emphasis is placed upon coaching, goal setting, and formalizing our processes and procedures. This approach relies on establishing the best *processes* and empowering people throughout our organization to implement and execute while using those processes.

I transitioned from my father's "top-down approach" to a "team-based, Servant Leadership" approach. This style of leadership places the owners and leaders at the bottom, serving our employees and helping them serve our customers, who are at the top.

My profile for a good leader would read like this: "Decisive servant leader . . . creative . . . capable of influencing people to work as a team and focus on common goals . . . produces extraordinary results through modeling the behaviors the company desires of its employees."

KEY LEADERSHIP ISSUE #1: BUILDING THE RIGHT TEAM

In my opinion, building a team begins with finding what my father called a "right-hand man."

Too often executives seem to search for a Dream Team. I believe the search should be focused on finding the right #2, a person who is capable, the right fit for what the business needs and certainly a person who can be trusted and is loyal. Find someone who can be honest with you, "as iron sharpens iron" (Proverbs 27:17). At the same time, find someone who complements your skills and personal attributes, filling in your weaknesses. I believe this is extremely important and rare. If you can find such a person, you will be strengthened, the synergy created will be incredible, and your company will benefit greatly.

I have such a man. His name is Mark Spuler, and we have worked together for thirty-seven years.

Mark and I met in 1968 when we were both leaving Philadelphia to attend Oral Roberts University. By the summer of 1972, we had both graduated and were back in Philly as friends, coworkers at CARDONE, and even brothers! I married Jacquie in 1969 and Mark married Jacquie's sister, Janeen, in 1971.

> *"Integrity includes but goes beyond honesty. Honesty is telling the truth—in other words,* conforming our words to reality. *Integrity is* conforming reality to our words*—in other words, keeping promises and fulfilling expectations. This requires an integrated character, a oneness primarily with self but also with life."*
>
> —STEPHEN COVEY, *THE 7 HABITS OF HIGHLY EFFECTIVE PEOPLE*

My father loved hiring and developing young talent with drive and potential, like Mark possesses. I don't mind telling you Dad was very disappointed and felt rejected when Mark and Janeen left us for a short time in the early 1970s to pursue missions work in Spain. The Spulers found their work with the people there fulfilling, but they also determined that they were not called to serve as full-time missionaries. When they returned to Philadelphia, there was a giant question between my father and Mark about whether he should return to CARDONE. My father had told Mark if he left the company to go to Spain, he wouldn't be allowed to come back to the company. It was one of the rare times when my father changed his mind, and I'm grateful that he did.

Time and time again, Mark has demonstrated not only tremendous skills and ability, but also flexibility. He has served CARDONE in many capacities and held many positions over the years, always willing to serve where needed. Today, he is our company's Chief Spiritual Officer, a Foundation Board Trustee, a gatekeeper of our culture globally, and a role model of a servant leader. Mark is savvy in business, with great accomplishments over the years, and all the while totally successful with people.

In many ways Mark and I have complementary skills. Our company has the Cardone name on it, but I know the company would not be what it is today without Mark.

This book would not have been written without Mark's insights, diligence, and follow-through. Mary Kay wrote in her book *You Can Have It All*, "Ideas are a dime a dozen, execution is priceless." I have certainly had ideas, but without Mark's energy, excellence, and faithful execution, we wouldn't be where we are as a business.

If you don't have a right-hand person you can trust, determine to find and develop one. Better yet, ask God to send you one.

KEY LEADERSHIP ISSUE #2: LAYING THE CORNERSTONE OF INTEGRITY

As I learned from my friends Ken Blanchard and Phil Hodges, there are four areas of our lives that result in our inner attitudes and our outer behaviors: our heart (our feelings), our head (our ideas and opinions), our hands (our actions), and our habits (our behavior patterns over time).[1] It is then that trust, loyalty, and productivity can be inspired in others. My goal as CEO of CARDONE is to get my own heart, head, hands, and habits aligned. And then, I want to encourage others around me, by both my words and my actions, to do the same. My desire is to see trust, loyalty, and productivity become the prevailing and ongoing atmosphere of our company.

TRUST: THE ESSENTIAL CORNERSTONE

Trust is very important to our employees and vital to me as a leader. There simply is no substitute for it. Trust begins to be established in saying what you mean and following through on what you say. The old saying, "A man is only as good as his word" is still true.

As CEO of CARDONE, I have a very strong sense that I *must* be a person others can trust if I ever hope to be a person that others will follow. One year, as we approached Christmas, I made a very costly mistake. After a very successful year, I announced at one of our company-wide meetings that CARDONE would be giving all of our Factory Family Members a Christmas bonus, specifying the amount.

After the meeting, I was quickly informed I had mistakenly stated a wrong and much higher amount than had been budgeted! I was shocked at what I had done, but I also knew what I had to do. I had to honor what I had said, even though I had been wrong. Failing to follow through on what I had said would have cost the company far more in terms of lost trust than it would cost to go ahead and pay the promised bonus.

I believe strongly it is important to do what we say and stand behind it, even when just one other person may be listening. A number of years ago I had a conversation with a well-known and distinguished CEO, who has led several major companies in our industry. In one of our discussions, I told him CARDONE would not create its own sales force, but would continue to rely on a network of independent sales representatives.

A few years after that conversation our market changed to the extent I had to make a new decision. I determined we needed our own factory-direct sales force to handle the customer consolidation and expanded product lines. I felt this issue was important enough for me to reverse my earlier decision. I also realized the right thing for me to do was to call him and explain my decision. He needed to know why I had changed my mind.

When we finally connected, I said, "I know this is what I told you before, but the business is changing and customers are requiring that we change. I wanted you to hear our decision straight from me." He listened, and then he thanked me for being up-front with him. He didn't necessarily agree with my decision, but he recognized my respect for him and the value I placed on my word. Thankfully, the trust between us was not broken.

ESTABLISHING A SPIRIT OF TRUST AND LABOR-MANAGEMENT COOPERATION

We wanted a relationship between labor and management built upon trust. Trust is a vital element in labor-management relationships. Trust is *the* key ingredient in an atmosphere of cooperation.

Cooperation is not only something we want to have within our company and factory walls; we want this same spirit of cooperation to extend to our neighbors, including the businesses, factories, and neighborhoods surrounding us. We always pursued nurturing that spirit of trust and cooperation; we want it to permeate all, including our relationship with our union.

As we started in business together, my father and I agreed we wanted a union in our business for the accountability it would bring. We wanted to care for our people, but if and when we erred, we knew the union would bring the error to our attention. The checks and balances gave us confidence we were leading correctly and doing right for our people.

Philadelphia was and still is a strong union town. It is not unusual for unions here to organize worker slowdowns or strikes to get their workers better wages or improved working conditions. Because of the mutual trust that has been built over the years between the union and our company, we have *never had a strike at CARDONE, nor have we ever come close to one.* Our union contracts have been unanimously approved without incident, because they are works of cooperation and mutual trust, which we have developed over many years.

What does a no-strike record mean to our Family Factory Members? It means they have an opportunity for continuous pay. Some of our workers have not missed a day of pay throughout their careers.

We've proven when people *trust* each other, they work together at a different and higher level that enables them to accomplish greater things. This is the way to effectively grow your business for the benefit of the customer. Our goal at CARDONE is to build relationships on trust.

QUESTIONS ONLY YOU CAN ANSWER

1. Do you have the right #2 person working with you?
2. What is the level of trust in your organization?

23

The Challenges Ahead

Who and What Will You Be Tomorrow?

Life is a journey—or as the Beatles put it, a "long and winding road." Nobody knows exactly where life will lead us or when it will end. The same is true for our businesses. We do our best to manage and plan, but we all know forces beyond our control and perhaps beyond anything we can imagine can change our world overnight.

While I am confident in the viability and growth of the remanufacturing industry, there are always changes as we view the external scan of our business environment. A revolutionary new technology, legislation affecting our business, an act of terrorism, war, or a natural disaster can happen and have an impact on our business.

Does this make me pessimistic? Not at all, because I believe that whatever happens there will always be opportunities available. Perhaps this is the very place where *faith* comes into full view for life and business.

Am I confident we are going to be smart enough to figure out the right thing to do in all cases? Am I confident our current business model will do as well in the future as it has in recent decades? Am I confident American industry will regain the position of global dominance it held in earlier times?

These are a few of the searching questions I have considered. Yet, I remain optimistic that by working hard and thinking creatively with other great people like the leaders in our company, including those in our operations around the world, we can reinvent ourselves as many times as necessary to develop a winning strategy, and we can do it not only for the next quarter, but for years to come.

> *"The world is moving so fast these days that the man who says it can't be done is generally interrupted by someone doing it."*[1]
>
> —HARRY EMERSON FOSDICK

Some of the challenges we face at CARDONE are unique to our business; other challenges we face are similar to the ones faced by all businesses. But I am committed to moving ahead with confidence and resolve and to give it my best shot.

THE CHALLENGE OF GLOBAL COMPETITION

American automobile manufacturers are facing major restructuring challenges to remain competitive. Buyouts and early retirement packages have been offered to tens of thousands of people in automotive-related industries in the last two years. Manufacturing facilities have been closed. None of this is good news for the automotive industry. It means the competition is increasingly fierce and profit margins in the automotive world are being impacted significantly and globally.

In Philadelphia, where we have our headquarters, manufacturers have eliminated 200,000 jobs in the past thirty years. From 1998 to 2006, U.S. manufacturers eliminated 3.4 million jobs.

During that same period, China's trade surplus with the United States grew from $57 billion to more than $201 billion.

Even in the automotive aftermarket, companies such as ours are no longer in competition with companies down the block or across the nation. We are competing globally against many foreign low-cost-labor companies, but we continue to reduce our costs, reinvent ourselves, and look for ways to remain competitive.

THE CHALLENGES RELATED TO PLANNING

We have been in business now for thirty-eight years. We started with five employees, and over the years we have always looked for opportunities, acted on them, and continued to find ways to grow. To most businesspeople's amazement, we did not have a strategic plan in those early years. Through the years we have made plans, but we have not placed high value on developing and executing a long-term strategic plan.

In years past, we worked with a major consulting firm to develop a five-year strategic plan. We spent considerable time and money constructing the plan. Then, with business conditions changing, we saw the plan become obsolete within a few months. Our plans had to change and change again.

> *"In times like these, it helps to recall that there have always been times like these."*[2]
>
> —PAUL HARVEY

As the pace of world business escalates, change escalates. Businesses have to be alert enough to see the shift and nimble enough to keep in step with the changes. Previously unimaginable or unforeseen business conditions can cause decisions in companies that affect our industry and create a ripple effect in our marketplace, requiring us to change and adjust our approach to doing business.

A key factor in CARDONE Industries' successful growth over the years has been our ability to plan, scan, recognize changes, and respond by altering our plans. The ability to quickly get our business back on track with unanimous focus on a common goal is of paramount importance. One of the major challenges the next generation at CARDONE will face will be the ability to develop effective plans. These plans must be extremely flexible, allowing for rapid adjustments as the global marketplace evolves and enabling our business to effectively adapt to those changes.

It seems to me there is a "psychological" problem that takes root once a plan has been developed. The plan tends to become an airtight, must-do guide for all decisions. How can a person truly look into the future and determine what must be done next year without change, much less five years down the line? When people begin to function according to a predetermined strategic plan, basing decisions on the plan they worked so hard to develop and are somewhat reluctant to change their plan, they tend to close themselves off from innovative solutions, creative ideas, and the ongoing flexibility that are necessary for adapting to a new environment and taking full advantage of new opportunities. Those who are tied to a plan are not dealing with the dynamics of the economy and market.

I look at plans as a guide or road map, which can be used to tell us where we want to go and how we want to get there. It is only right, however, to change the plan if the assumptions and external scans warrant it.

To me, the only thing about a man-made plan that can be determined with total accuracy and precision is our man-made plans are *never* going to be totally accurate. The orders are never going to come in exactly to plan and the numbers are never going to be in total alignment with the projections.

I hope that we at CARDONE never get locked into any plan to the degree we are not willing to change it, creatively. And those associated with the planning functions should show flexibility throughout the process of developing and implementing the plan.

The biblical account of David meeting Goliath illustrates a great lesson related to planning. David had a plan. He selected five smooth stones, but with God, David only used one stone. I believe we need to plan, but we should also leave room for God in our plans.

On a fairly recent trip to Israel I learned another tremendous lesson about planning. When making a statement about the future, an Israeli typically lifts his hand, puts up his little finger, and says, "But God . . ." This signifies the person's belief that God can have an impact on both the plan and the outcome. In my planning, I always want to leave room for God.

THE CHALLENGE OF SUCCESSION

As indicated briefly in a previous chapter, one of the great challenges of a family-owned business is the challenge of succession. This challenge, of course, is not only one for family-owned businesses. Every company faces the challenge of determining who will eventually take over the existing reins of leadership.

Before turning over the leadership of the company, my father worked long and hard in developing me for this role. I find myself doing the same thing now. Today, I know more than any other person how much I did to prepare and qualify for the position and honor of leading CARDONE Industries. I don't think any person should be given a position or title if the person is incapable or unqualified.

My son, Michael, is working hard to learn the business. He has a vision for the future, which has already impacted our global expansion. Michael started working for CARDONE when he was thirteen. He has earned his MBA in International Management from Thunderbird School of Global Management. Michael led the team that established CARDONE Industries Europe. He led the team that began our remanufacturing operations in Matamoras, Mexico, and he has worked in and led virtually all parts of our business during his career at CARDONE Industries.

"My protection and success comes from God alone.
He is my refuge, a rock where no enemy can reach me."
—PSALM 62:7 TLB

After earning his undergraduate degree in engineering, my son-in-law, Dan, earned a Master of Business Administration degree from Drexel University. When he joined our company, he was given engineering responsibilities and led various operations at our Philadelphia manufacturing facilities. Then, he and his family moved to Belgium for five years, where Dan served as the Managing Director of CARDONE Industries Europe. Today Dan leads our global engineering team.

Both Michael and Dan are talented leaders who have worked

and developed within our business. They have earned the respect and confidence of others at CARDONE Industries. These two servant leaders are fully committed to our culture and are excellent role models for the next generation.

Today, I am CEO and Chairman of the Board at CARDONE. In 2005, the board appointed the first non-family president in the company's history, and he still serves in that role today. Although it is our desire to remain family-owned, it will be the board's decision to always seek out and determine the best individuals to lead the company, whether they are or are not family members.

What I have learned is this: if your goal is to maintain a family-owned, professionally run business with family members involved in the day-to-day running of the business, you have to plan and make preparations in advance. Make sure family members are thoroughly prepared and well trained with adequate exposure and experience. Then, develop a succession plan and always seek the *most* qualified person for each position in your business.

THE CHALLENGE OF RAPID CHANGE

We are all aware of the rapid rate of change in our world. Everyone faces a tremendous challenge to keep up and personally adapt to change, sometimes daily, so it seems.

In these changing times, I believe our values are what give us firm footing, enabling us to stand on solid ground in the face of a shifting and uncertain future. Our values are like a compass, which helps to keep us on track. Values are our "True North."

Leadership that remains true and rooted in values can ride the waves of change.

On the other hand, valueless leaders are blown by the winds of change. Without a true sense of direction, they make valueless judgments based on short-term goals, personal gain, and what seems right at the time. And that is not leadership at all!

Trends to Consider

There are a number of trends that are worth considering when discussing spiritual issues and their relevance to and impact upon the workplace. Consider the following trends:

- People are spending longer and longer hours at work.
- People are aware moral breakdown not only impacts morale in their workplace, but it can also lead to the demise of a company.
- Americans seem to be increasingly assertive about their right to express their faith in public; some have even pursued legal actions against employers who inhibited their ability to express their faith at work.
- The water cooler has become the new "international relations" public square at many companies, a place where people of many different cultures interact daily.
- More and more companies are feeling a need to set guidelines for appropriate and inappropriate religious discourse in the workplace.

As a CEO, my greatest desire is to live out my values at home and work. While my faith and values do not guarantee CARDONE will never fail or that we will be successful at all times, they do give me dir... rpose. My faith continually serves to remind ... g, no, make that Someone, who is much big- ... lone Jr., running this universe. God gives me ... l confidence we can continue to make a dif-

...NLY YOU CAN ANSWER

... your personal major challenges in

... he major challenges facing your

... g tomorrow's challenges *today*?

NOTES

Chapter 2

1. Peter F. Drucker with Joseph A. Maciariello, *The Daily Drucker* (New York: HarperCollins), page 16.

Chapter 3

1. Ken Blanchard and Phil Hodges, *The Servant Leader* (Nashville: Thomas Nelson Publishers), pages 26–29.

Chapter 4

1. Tom Chappell, *Managing Upside Down* (New York: William Morrow and Co.).

Chapter 5

1. Drucker and Maciariello, *The Daily Drucker*, page 301.

Chapter 6

1. Rebecca Goldin, "Counting the Cost of Stress," *New York Times* (September 23, 2004).

Chapter 7

1. Drucker and Maciariello, *The Daily Drucker*, page 108.
2. Quoted by C. William Pollard in *The Soul of the Firm* (Grand Rapids, Mich.: Zondervan), page 25.
3. Author unknown.

Chapter 8

1. Quoted by Jim Collins in *Good to Great* (New York: HarperBusiness), page 51.

Chapter 9

1. U.S. motor vehicle population data from R. L. Polk & Co., in Automotive Aftermarket Industry Association's *Digital Aftermarket Factbook 2010.*
2. Facts from Rolf Steinhilper, *Remanufacturing: The Ultimate Form of Recycling* (Germany: Fraunhofer IRB Verlag, 1998); and Robert T. Lund, *The Remanufacturing Industry: Hidden Giant* (Boston: Boston University, 1996).

3. Sharon Hoffman, *The G.I.F.T.ED Woman* (Colorado Springs, Colo.: David C. Cook, 2004), page 219.

CHAPTER 10

1. "Absenteeism and the Bottom Line," *Braun Consulting Newsletter* (November 28, 2007, Volume 7, Number 4).
2. Graham S. Lowe, Ph.D., "Healthy Workplace Strategies" (Kelowna, British Columbia: The Graham Lowe Group & Health Canada, January 2004).

CHAPTER 11

1. Jennifer Caban, "Michael Dell and the Success of Dell Inc." (www.AssociatedContent.com, June 5, 2007).

CHAPTER 12

1. You can read more about how Toyota takes their culture of excellence around the world in the book *The Toyota Way* by Jeffrey Liker (New York: McGraw-Hill).
2. From *Japan Quality Control Circles* (Tokyo: Asian Productivity Organization, Edition 3, 1983).

CHAPTER 13

1. "Absenteeism and the Bottom Line," *Braun Consulting News*, page 3.
2. We calculate that it costs CARDONE about $7,500 to replace an employee. In one recent year, the Spiritual Life department addressed 391 conflict resolution cases. Conservatively speaking, about 25 percent of such cases (or 98 cases) result in termination without chaplain intervention. We want to avoid those terminations.
3. Chaplains provided pastoral care, referrals, coordination of emergency and nonemergency transportation, and translation services in 6,999 cases directly related to problems resulting in employees leaving work early, coming to work late, or being absent from work. The average time spent on each of these conflict-resolution cases was five hours.

CHAPTER 14

1. Quoted in Joseph A. Michelli, *The Starbucks Experience* (New York: McGraw-Hill), page 7.
2. Author unknown.

CHAPTER 16

1. Peter F. Drucker, *The Essential Drucker* (New York: Harper Paperbacks), page 21.

CHAPTER 17

1. Keith H. Hammonds, "We, Incorporated," *Fast Company* (December 19, 2007), online.

CHAPTER 18

1. "Bad News for Bullies," *U.S. News & World Report* (June 19, 2006), page 54.
2. You can read more about upending the leadership pyramid model in these business tales: Ken Jennings and John Stahl-Wert, *The Serving Leader* (San Francisco: Berrett-Koehler Publishers, Inc.) and James C. Hunter, *The Servant* (New York: Crown Business).
3. Ken Blanchard and Phil Hodges, *The Servant Leader* (Nashville: Thomas Nelson Publishers), pages 17–18.

CHAPTER 19

1. Phil Hodges, *Lead Like Jesus Participant Workbook* (Augusta, Ga.: Center for Faithwalk Leadership), page 7.

CHAPTER 20

1. Joseph H. Astrachan and Melissa Carey Shanker, "Family Businesses' Contribution to the U.S. Economy: A Closer Look," *Family Business Review*, vol. XVI, no. 3 (Family Firm Institute, Inc., September 2003), pages 211–19.
2. Special report in *Business Week* titled "Family Inc." by Joseph Weber in Chicago and Louis Lavelle in New York, with Tom Lowry in New York, Wendy Zellner in Dallas, Amy Barrett in Philadelphia, and bureau reports (November 10, 2003).

CHAPTER 21

1. Quoted by Gary Moore in *Faithful Finances 101* (West Conshohocken, Penn.: Templeton Press).

CHAPTER 22

1. Ken Blanchard and Phil Hodges, *Lead Like Jesus* (Nashville: Thomas Nelson Publishers).

CHAPTER 23

1. Quoted by Dr. Norman Vincent Peale in *You Can If You Think You Can* (New York: Fireside), page 116.
2. Quoted by Marianne M. Jennings in *A Business Tale* (New York: AMACOM, a division of American Management Association), page 95.

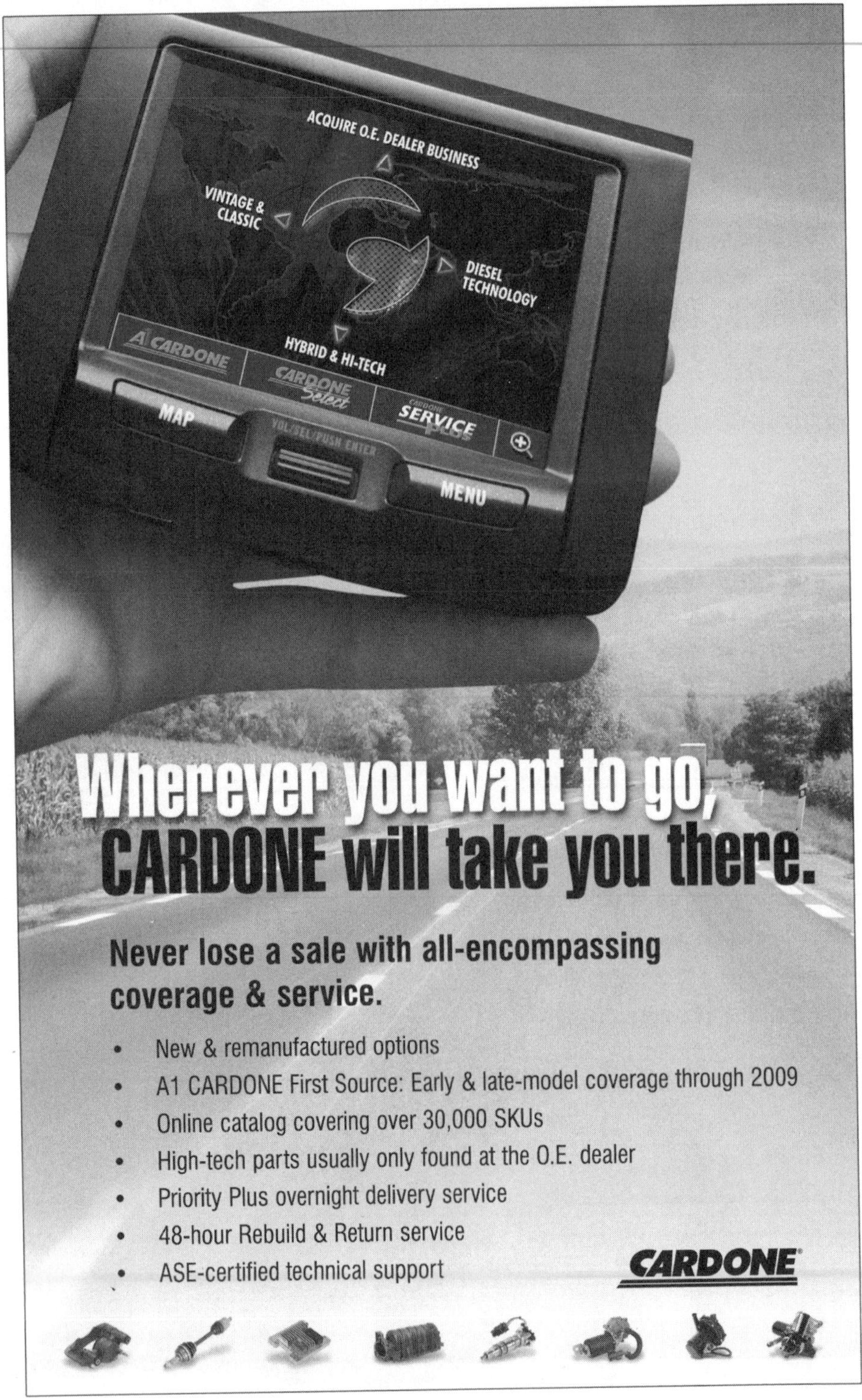
ACQUIRE O.E. DEALER BUSINESS
VINTAGE & CLASSIC
DIESEL TECHNOLOGY
HYBRID & HI-TECH
A1 CARDONE
CARDONE Select
CARDONE SERVICE PLUS
MAP
VOL/SEL/PUSH ENTER
MENU
Wherever you want to go,
CARDONE will take you there.
Never lose a sale with all-encompassing coverage & service.
• New & remanufactured options
• A1 CARDONE First Source: Early & late-model coverage through 2009
• Online catalog covering over 30,000 SKUs
• High-tech parts usually only found at the O.E. dealer
• Priority Plus overnight delivery service
• 48-hour Rebuild & Return service
• ASE-certified technical support
CARDONE

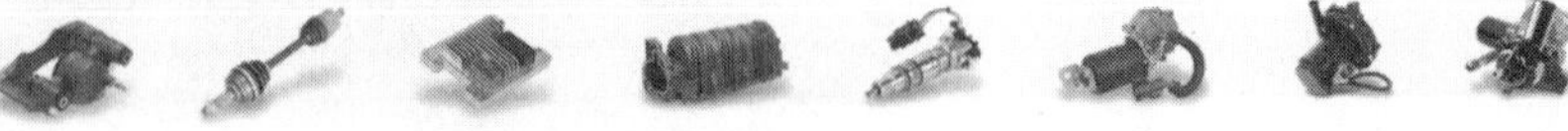